RETHINKING THE
CLASSROOM
LANDSCAPE

Creating Environments That
Connect Young Children,
Families, and Communities

Sandra Duncan, EdD, Jody Martin, and Rebecca Kreth

Gryphon House
www.gryphonhouse.com

Published by Gryphon House, Inc.
P. O. Box 10, Lewisville, NC 27023
800.638.0928; 877.638.7576 (fax)
Visit us on the web at www.gryphonhouse.com.

Reprinted September 2019

Bulk Purchase
Gryphon House books are available for special premiums and sales promotions as well as for fund-raising use. Special editions or book excerpts also can be created to specifications. For details, call 800.638.0928.

Disclaimer
Gryphon House, Inc., cannot be held responsible for damage, mishap, or injury incurred during the use of or because of activities in this book. Appropriate and reasonable caution and adult supervision of children involved in activities and corresponding to the age and capability of each child involved are recommended at all times. Do not leave children unattended at any time. When making choices about allowing children to touch or eat certain foods, plants, or flowers, make sure to investigate possible toxicity and consider any food allergies or sensitivities. Observe safety and caution at all times.

Library of Congress Cataloging-in-Publication Data
Names: Duncan, Sandra., 1945- author. | Martin, Jody, author. | Kreth,
    Rebecca, author.
Title: Rethinking the classroom landscape : creating environments that
    connect young children, families, and communities / Sandra Duncan, EdD,
    Jody Martin, Rebecca Kreth.
Description: Lewisville, NC : Gryphon House, Inc., [2016]
Identifiers: LCCN 2016023945 | ISBN 9780876595633
Subjects: LCSH: Classroom environment. | Early childhood
    education--Environmental aspects.
Classification: LCC LB3013 .D855 2016 | DDC 371.102/4--dc23 LC record available at https://lccn.loc.gov/2016023945

Acknowledgments

- - - - - - - - - - - -

We want to extend our deepest appreciation and gratitude to those who shared knowledge, insight, and inspiration for this book: children and teachers in the exemplary classrooms, centers, and schools represented, early childhood advocates who graciously shared their personal stories, early childhood companies that provided images and ideas about naturally inspired products, college students who offered fresh innovative thinking, and colleagues who guided us with their wisdom. And finally, to our friends and families, we thank you for supporting, encouraging, and giving us the time and latitude to write this book. For all, we are deeply grateful.

Sue Penix • Downtown Baltimore Child Care • Dr. Pradnya Patet • Mountain Road Preschool • Dana Wiser • TalTree Arboretum • Danielle Monroy • Liana Chavarin • Nature Explore • Dr. Ruth Wilson • Natural Pod • Rhonda Johnson • Nancy Rosenow • Pressman Academy Early Childhood Center • Rachel Larimore • Creative Care for Children • Nancy Manewith • Early Learning Children's Community • Gail Szautner • Piper Center for Family Studies at Baylor University • Life Without Plastic • Celeste Joyner • Carri McGuire • Chippewa Nature Center's Nature Preschool • Crystal Sanders • Mickey MacGillivray • Early Learning Children's Community • Kay Koern • Vyvyan Carver • Creative Child Care Center • Steve Erwin • Danielle Werchuk • College of the Canyons Early Childhood Center • Nancy Alexander • County Child Care • Dawn McCloud • Bellaboo's Children's Play and Discovery Center • Milestones Early Childhood Development Center • Happy Faces II Academy • Lisa Krueger • Alexander Graham Bell Montessori School • John Rosenow • Child Development and Learning Laboratory • Amarie Merasty • Opportunity School • Dr. Gerald Newmark • Coyote Trails School of Nature • The Children's Project • Dimensions Education Program • Just for You • Glenn Smith • Children's Choice • Louise Mass • Mykaela Haarstad • Christa Winters • Kimberly Greene Epps • Ganero Child Development Center at Pierce College • Margo Sipes • Eric Strickland • Board of Jewish Early Education Center at B'nai Tikvah • Sydney Roach • City Neighbors • Sherry Trebus • Courtney Gardner • Hope's Home • Janet Sear • Place of our Own • Children's Home + Aid •

Milgard Child Development Center at Pierce College • Lakisha Reid • Mountain Road Preschool • Tammy Lockwood • Talkeetna Child Development Center • Cindi Catlin Gaskins • Gretchen House • Cookie Cummings • The Nature Preschool at Irvine Nature Center • Sharyl Robin • Community Playthings • Margaret Desmores • The Children's College • Children's Discovery Museum • Corinne Lagoy • Monica Wiedel-Lubinski • The Adventure Club • Chief Leschi Schools Preschool Programs • Nancy W. Darden Child Development Center at East Carolina University • Kathy Walker • Discovery Early Learning Center • Jeremy South • Steilacoom Family Center • Katie Gilstad • Rebecca Stoessner • Growing Minds Learning Center • Julie Fowler • Nature's Way Preschool • Jacquelyn Weller • Winnetka Public Schools • Marcus Collins • Barbara McVicker • The Saul Spielberg Early Childhood Center • Corrine Tollett-Carr • Region 16 Head Start • Monica Walker • Erin Austria • Care for Tots Learning Center • Jay Sinha • United States Air Force Child Development Centers • Heather Parker • Lynn Hummel • Roslyn Outdoor School • Dr. Debarati Majumdar Narayan • Treezles • Paula Barnes • Board of Jewish Education Early Childhood Centers at Beth Hillel • Special Blessings Child Care • City Neighbors Hamilton • Bridgitte Alomes • Peifer Elementary School • Sue Noble • Valerie Caswell • Denika Hucks • CASA Child Care • Berkeley Forest School • Mari Potter • Little Explorers • University Presbyterian Children's Center • Daniel Robert • Midland Children's Discovery Museum • Rae Pica • Creative Care for Children • Forest Ridge Academy • Community Play School

Contents

Preface

– – – – –

Children are miracles. Believing that every child is a miracle can transform the way we design for children's care. When we invite a miracle into our lives we prepare ourselves and the environment around us . . . . We make it our job to create, with reverence and gratitude, a space that is worthy of a miracle!

—Anita Rui Olds, *Child Care Design Guide*

Is your space worthy? If we blindfolded you, took you on a plane, and dropped you in the middle of an early childhood classroom, would you know where you are based on what you see? Our premise is the answer would be "no" because most classrooms look the same. The majority of materials and equipment now found in most early childhood classrooms are specified and manufactured for early childhood environments. The result: cookie-cutter classrooms.

Rethinking the Classroom Landscape encourages teachers of young children to transform ordinary spaces into reflective and meaningful landscapes. With easy-to-implement ideas and strategies based on five guideposts, this book supports and encourages educators to create early childhood environments that vividly connect to children, adults, and their communities. We believe in the importance of neighborhood and communities, the connection between past and present with the people who live in these communities, and the influence of geography, topography, flora, and fauna. We believe that early childhood environments should be not just the actual spaces and objects within these spaces, but also a reflection of the geographical, cultural, historical, and environmental forces shaping these spaces. We believe in the important distinction between space and place.

It is our hope that after reading this book and seeing the beautiful images of classrooms across the country, teachers will rid themselves of the cookie-cutter mentality and become curators of classroom landscapes that honor the miracles in our lives.

—Sandra Duncan, Jody Martin, and Rebecca Kreth

Introduction: Guideposts for Children's Landscapes

If you don't know where you're from, you'll have a hard time saying where you're going.

—Wendell Berry

The Power of the Environment

Space speaks. Even though we cannot hear the classroom's walls or floors talking, the equipment conversing, or the learning materials chattering, they are, indeed, speaking to us. They are telling us how to behave, act, react, engage, and even think. The space is whispering "run" or "pause and linger for a while." Not only is the space speaking to our physical beings, it is speaking to our emotions and our senses, as Jim Greenman notes in his book *Caring Spaces, Learning Spaces*. Physical objects speak and let us know if they can be touched and explored . . . or if they are off limits. Furniture in the space and the way it is arranged silently speaks by influencing our behaviors and controlling our emotions. The physical environment is indeed very powerful. The environment, however, is more than the physical setting within the classroom's four walls.

1

Architect Mark Dudek defined the classroom environment as an evolving landscape for children's exploration and play within the four walls and beyond. Environment is not only the actual spaces and the objects within it, but also the social and cultural forces that shape the space—and are in turn shaped by those who use them. American heritage farmer and poet Wendell Barry believes our environments—both indoors and outdoors—connect us to where we are and translate into who we are in powerful ways. So it is with the landscapes we create for young children.

For many of us, the classroom is defined as four surrounding walls and the accompanying floor, a few doors, some windows, and perhaps children's bathrooms, storage areas, and preparation spaces. As architect Dudek pointed out, however, a classroom environment should be considered as much, much more. In addition to the physical structure, the environment includes the land on which the structure is built. The environment is the natural geography, topography, flora, and fauna. It includes the local neighborhood and a mosaic of cultures living within the community. The environment consists of the community's past and present . . . its traditions, food, and music. The classroom environment is about relationships and connections within and outside the classroom walls. Its landscape is both visible and invisible, finite and infinite, and a powerful influence on children's growth and development. For this reason, it is important to have guidelines for designing children's landscapes.

Guidepost 1

Create an Environment Worthy of Its Inhabitants

As early childhood educators, it is our responsibility to ensure that young children develop into their highest potential. In doing so, we also need to examine and expect the same from ourselves so that in the context of transforming our classroom environments, we are also changing and transforming ourselves as educators. Just as with children, we personally must strive to reach beyond our limits and embrace our true potential. We must welcome change and the opportunities it brings . . . for in doing so, we recognize the unique and diverse attributes of each child and adult who makes up the human landscape of our classrooms. We must create an environment worthy of its inhabitants.

Guidepost 2

Meet the Basic Needs of All Children in Their Environments

Young children are in the process of becoming their best self. Full of life, innocence, and wonder, children bring their whole selves and basic needs to our classrooms. Meeting these critical and important needs in their first learning environment is a remarkable opportunity for early learning professionals. Because we are ultimately responsible for shaping our classroom environments, it is important to create spaces where children feel welcome, included, secure, and experience a sense of belonging.

Guidepost 3

Provide Authentic Play Places for Young Children

Children are born creative beings and inherently wired to play. Their most natural state of being is playing. Each classroom moment is an exciting creative play opportunity for children to learn about their immediate worlds. It becomes important, then, to regard the landscapes of our classrooms as blank pallets—somewhat like theater stages—where children perform and act out their daily lives. The children are the performers and we are the stage directors. It is our responsibility, as effective stage directors, to offer authentic props and materials designed to transform children's creative play into intricate stories of their lives.

Guidepost 4

Connect Children to Community

Children are a reflection of their communities. Children's lives are enriched by understanding they are an important part of their local neighborhoods and communities. This important understanding has a positive impact on how children view their own abilities to influence their worlds. If we believe this to be true, then it is critically necessary to create a strong connection between the classroom and children's neighborhoods, communities, and the people who live within.

Guidepost 5

Naturalize Children's Environments

Nature is the natural teacher for all of humankind. Children's connection to nature is primary, timeless, and sacred. As educators, we must tap into this innate enthusiasm about the natural world. Providing ample outside time as well as infusing natural elements indigenous from your community into the classroom strengthens and stimulates children's physical, cognitive, and emotional growth. It is our definitive responsibility to diligently and continually cultivate children's personal relationships with the land, which will sustain their energies, wonder, and memories for a lifetime.

1

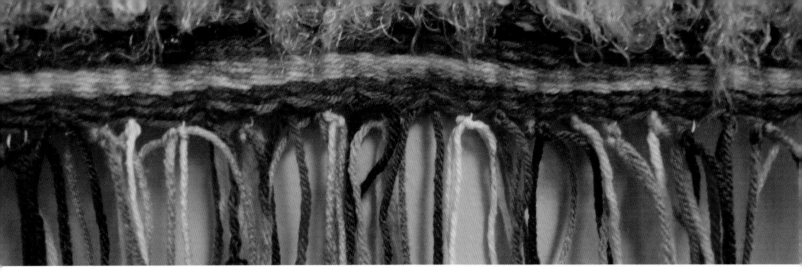

Alexander Graham Bell Montessori School (Wheeling, Illinois)

The Classroom Tapestry

An invisible red thread connects those who are destined to meet regardless of time, place, or circumstances.
The red thread may stretch or tangle, but it will never break.

—Ancient Chinese proverb

Tapestry of Life

There is an invisible thread of life that connects us all. It weaves in and out among us to create a unique tapestry of beauty and diversity. Beginning with the child and radiating out to the family, school, and community, this invisible thread joins us all together. This thread entwines everything and everyone—creating a tapestry of interdependency and interconnection impossible to unravel.

Imagine this tapestry with many threads of various colors weaving in and out—forming patterns of colors and shapes—creating a beautiful piece of art. Traditionally, a tapestry is woven on a loom where there are two sets of interlaced threads, those running parallel to the length and those running parallel to the width. As the colored threads are woven back and forth, the combining colors create new colors and shades. Each single colored thread connects with another thread to create a pattern. They are bound together; they all connect.

Life is much like a tapestry. Life is filled with people, places, experiences, and relationships—all interwoven with many cross threads binding us all together. Just as a tapestry is filled with fibers and layers of various textures, so is the world in which we live. Some of the fibers are rough; some are smooth. The threads are of many tones of colors—all beautiful and all unique. Some colors complement, while others dramatically clash. Yet when intricately woven together, the differences disappear and the tapestry's lavish beauty appears. Eminent psychologist Urie Bronfenbrenner understood life's tapestry and the importance of interconnectedness when he proposed the human ecological theory of children's development.

Similar to the assortment of threads in an intricately woven tapestry, the lives of young children also include numerous and varied threads or environments such as family, school, peers, and community. The ground on which we walk, schools we attend, and retail establishments in the community we frequent are all common denominators. The relationships we have with each other within these physical locations are the connecting denominators. It is the interconnectedness of these threads that create the tapestries of young children's lives.

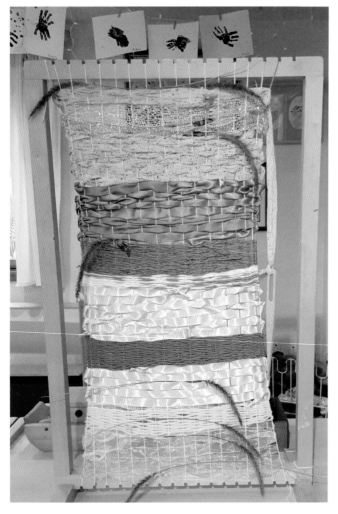

Creative Care for Children (Santa Barbara, California)

Bronfenbrenner's Tapestry and Its Threads

The general framework for this book is based on Bronfenbrenner's ecological model of human development, which involves interrelationships between humans and their environments. Surrounded by these complex systems of relationships, the child's development is affected by multiple tapestry threads. These interrelated threads include—but extend beyond—home, school, and community environments in which young children live. Bronfenbrenner's model provides the whole picture of the developing child by taking into consideration the powerful influences of five systems in which relationships and interactions form patterns that affect human development. These systems include the microsystem, mesosystem, exosystem, macrosystem, and chronosystem. Woven together, they become the tapestry of life.

- **Microsystem.** The child's interactions and relationships with people or objects in the immediate environment make up this system. Positive and supportive interactions are naturally important to a child's growth.
- **Mesosystem.** This system refers to how two individuals or groups immediately affecting the child interact with one another. Nearest the child is the family system. The family is an ever-changing social system in which members continually adapt to address one another's needs. Many life transitions, such as the birth of a child, a new job for the mother, and beginning school, all contribute to interactions that can affect a child's development. Also likely to influence development are the educational or care systems, including the relationships within and among these environments. Communication between the child's family and school is an example of a mesosystem. The quality of the positive communications and relationships between school and home supports the growth and development of the child. When these links are strong, there is likely to be more growth in all

Community Play School (Baltimore, Maryland)

developmental areas, including the child's academic competence.

- **Exosystem.** The exosystem refers to environments in which the young child is not always an active participant, but is affected in one or more systems or environments. This system includes social services, school and community boards, parents' employment, extended family, and mass media. A parent, for example, may work in a family-friendly company that allows flexibility in work hours so a parent can attend

The larger circle represents our classroom community. The many values, cultures, ideas, and perspectives of the parents, children, and teachers are intertwined to create a diverse community that we call Preschool 1. Our goal is for all voices to be heard and accepted, working together to provide a collaborative community for us all to be a part of.

Early Learning Children's Community (Lansing, Michigan)

center or school functions, provides employer-supported child care, or offers extended school care.

- **Macrosystem.** The macrosystem setting consists of the society and subculture in which the child belongs. The macrosystem includes belief systems, socio-economic status, patterns of social interaction, and lifestyles. Examples of macrosystems include the country of the United States, ethnic ancestry, socio-economic factors, urban or rural living conditions, and religious beliefs. These larger characteristics of society influence the child's development. A child, for example, born to a family living in poverty in a rural area experiences life in a much different way than a child born to an affluent family living in New York City.

- **Chronosystem.** The chronosystem includes the transitions experienced during a person's lifetime. A classic example is divorce, which is a major transition for the parents and the child. Although the divorce definitely affects the parents' relationships, the breakup also potentially affects the child's behavior and social-emotional development. The chronosystem includes historical experiences and present-day experiences as well. As an example, parents in the 1940s were concerned about polio, but today's parents may be more concerned about public and personal safety.

Bronfenbrenner's ecological theory includes many different systems thought to impact children's development, and he believed that these systems or circles of influence act in tandem. Each system has an invisible thread that winds in and out among us—from one environment to the other—just like a beautiful tapestry. Like the artisan who focuses on the tapestry's intricacies and patterns, it is equally important for teachers creating and designing classroom landscapes to focus on the intersection and powerful influences of the threads in children's lives.

Newmark's Five Critical Emotional Needs of Childhood

The child is at the center of this tapestry of life envisioned by Bronfenbrenner. As young children develop, their environments and accompanying experiences become embedded in the architecture of their brains. According to the National Scientific Council on the Developing Child's 2011 research, children who have positive emotional experiences have a greater sense of belonging. Whether at home, in the community, or at school, children need to feel that they have an authentic role to play in these environments. This means children must be viewed and listened to as important people with individual and important needs, according to teacher educators Ellen Lynn Hall and Jennifer Kofkin Rudkin.

In the book *How to Raise Emotionally Healthy Children: Meeting the Five Critical Needs of Children . . . and Parents Too*, Gerald Newmark highlights the critical emotional needs of young children.

- **Respected.** For children to feel respected, they need to be treated in a courteous, thoughtful, attentive, and civil manner. Children crave to be considered as individuals who are deserving of the same courtesy and consideration as others.

- **Important.** Children need to believe they are an important force in the world. They must be of these opinions: I have value. I am useful. I have power. I am somebody.

- **Accepted.** For children to feel accepted, they need to be assured that they have a right to their own feelings, opinions, ideas, concerns, wants, and needs. Regardless of their physical or cognitive capabilities, children are their own unique individuals.

- **Included.** Children need to feel that they belong, are part of the environment, are connected to other people, and can make important and significant contributions to their group.

- **Secure.** For children, security means creating a positive and consistent environment where people care about one another and show it through their actions and words. Although the physical structure exists for children to feel safe and protected, there is enough flexibility and freedom for children to actively participate and influence the world in which they live.

We know children do not develop in a vacuum. Rather, their development is connected to many different systems. All these different systems or environments—such as family, school, and community—interconnect to create the tapestry of young children's lives.

As a teacher, you might be wondering how you can create an environment that reflects Bronfenbrenner's ecological theory of child development. What can you do to promote interrelationships and magnify connections to the classroom with parents and the community? How can you use Newmark's five critical needs to redesign and strengthen your classroom's tapestry? You will find many creative and meaningful ideas in the sections that follow.

Community Play School's Core Values

Because children deserve to . . .

- Be emotionally safe
- Be known as individuals
- Show all emotions
- Feel brave
- Have authentic relationships
- Be children
- Have privacy, materials, choice, and responsibility
- Have respect
- Be heard
- Wonder
- Have empathy/compassion
- Have supervision
- Feel powerful
- Be capable

We . . .

- See them as human beings with aspirations, shortcomings, abilities, and feelings
- Trust that children do things for valid reasons
- Create curriculum together
- Approach each situation individually
- Support and nurture them
- Guide them
- Give them time and space
- Give them freedom and responsibility
- Give them interesting provocations
- Provide a variety of approaches

We believe . . .

- In materials and environments that create wonder, choice, ownership, privacy, and idleness (environmental)
- That children construct their own knowledge of themselves, others, and the world, through experience, time, and space (cognitive)
- In building strong relationships and connections between children and adults (and within themselves) (social-emotional)
- In children's physical well-being (physical)
- In the importance of child development and intentional interactions with individuals (role of teacher)
- That childhood is in danger and in need of protection (advocacy)

Strengthening Your Classroom Tapestry

Bronfenbrenner's model and the critical emotional needs outlined by Newmark focus on the child first and foremost, and then consider the influences of other elements or threads in a child's life. For example, one of the ways children can learn about respect is to know how it feels to be respected by observing parents or teachers treating each other in a respectful way (teacher and family thread). When the teacher allows children to design their own spaces, it helps them feel important (teacher and child thread). Accepting children as individuals in their own right with their own uniqueness as well as representing families in the classroom environment helps them feel accepted (child and family thread). Bringing in artifacts and natural

objects from the local community or neighborhood offers opportunities for children to experience and understand their immediate world (child and community thread). These personal contributions and collaborations help children feel included. Security means the teacher creates a positive environment where children can be children, and their differences are not only accepted but rejoiced and celebrated. In a secure environment, enough structure exists for children to feel safe and protected, yet the environment provides opportunities for challenges, choices, and taking chances (teacher and child thread).

To create a strong classroom environment, it is important to be aware of each of the important threads in your classroom. Incorporate Bronfenbrenner's model and Newmark's five critical emotional needs into your classroom's tapestry. By intentionally including their theories and ideas, you can weave a beautiful tapestry taking into consideration the interrelationships of humans and their environment as well as the critical needs that must be met for children to succeed. Take a look at the following ideas for strengthening your classroom's tapestry with the child, family, and community threads.

Child's Thread

Welcome stones. Each child has a unique stone to call his own, which helps the child feel important. As a parent and child enter the classroom, they find the child's name on one of the stones and place it in the basket. Placing the stone in the basket symbolizes the transfer from the family to the classroom. The child feels secure and included, knowing that he is part of a larger group of children who have also placed their stones in the basket.

The Nature Preschool at Irvine Nature Center (Owings Mills, Maryland)

Child Development and Learning Laboratory at Central Michigan University (Mount Pleasant, Michigan)

Milgard Child Development Center at Pierce College (Lakewood, Washington)

Invitation to come in. Placing a collection of interesting and intentionally organized materials in a location visible from the classroom's door sparks a child's curiosity. Igniting children's motivation to come in, these evocative objects send a message of welcome to entering children, making them feel secure in the transition from the home to school.

Hint: Consider including an invitation area as part of your permanent classroom arrangement. Positioned near the classroom's entry, this area could be a small table, shelf, or rug. Emulate children's museums by offering objects that draw young children like magnets and trigger their active engagement and natural

curiosity. By continually refreshing the objects and making the area feel new, you can ensure that the invitation area always pulls in children.

My house. Including photographs of children's homes in the classroom creates a classroom connection and sends a message to children that they and their families are important and respected. Placing a framed picture of a child's home in the construction area, for example, encourages children to design and construct their classmate's home from the blocks and building materials. Having framed pictures of children's homes in the writing area promotes conversation, story making, and journal entries. Displaying an image of a child's home near the easel also encourages children to re-create the home with paints.

Collaborative artistry. Give children a chance to be artistic in a shared way and have their work displayed. This child was one of the artisans who felt important and included as he carefully selected and then wove ribbon, beads, and colorful strands of thread through the chicken wire, which was invitingly placed on a nearby table. After children experienced the textures and colors of the weaving materials, the beautiful tapestry was displayed on the classroom wall for all to see and enjoy.

I'm here! Children feel important when they are asked to find their names as part of the morning ritual. By sticking their names in the pumpkin, children have an active and visual way to feel included. Accomplished with the help of parents, this activity helps children transition from the security of parents' arms to the preschool classroom.

Hint: After the pumpkin has been used for a while, it becomes poked full of holes. Try placing the pumpkin outside to see what creatures might come visit and check it out.

Children's Choice (Prince Albert, Saskatchewan, Canada)

Chippewa Nature Center's Nature Preschool (Midland, Michigan)

Transitioning activity. You can position a basket of shells (or pinecones, rocks, or leaves) outside the classroom door. Before entering, the child selects a shell, brings it into the classroom, and places it in another basket just inside the door. This daily ritual helps children feel secure and included in the classroom community.

Little One Family Center (Boston, Massachusetts)

Rethinking the Classroom Landscape

Family's Thread

Family puzzles. To honor the uniqueness of children and families, you can offer a blank puzzle piece to adults and children to create drawings showcasing their personalities. Each piece displays the adult's or child's creativity using vibrant colors, playful characters, and abstract drawings. The individual pieces can be put back together to form a unified picture highlighting a sense of community among all the families and children in the center.

Early Learning Children's Community (Lansing, Michigan)

You belong. Soft lighting, a sheer fabric drape, an inspirational quote, and natural elements are inviting and cozy as children and their families are welcomed into the classroom, helping them not only to feel included and secure, but to believe that they belong right here in this beautiful spot.

Our memories. Children and families write down their favorite memories of the school year, which are posted in the hallway. Displaying notes from children and their families in an area where parents gather creates a sense of belonging. Children and parents see themselves and others represented, which gives a feeling of acceptance of each child's individuality.

Nature's Way Preschool (Kalamazoo, Michigan)

Tiny Tot Preschool (Houston, Texas)

Make it a family affair. Acknowledge all the men in your children's lives by requesting they bring in a man's tie—it doesn't matter if the tie belonged to grandpa, dad, uncle, brother, neighbor, or friend. Everyone will feel important and part of the ceremony as they honor the special man in their lives. Use women's scarves for a similar display of honor.

Hint: For displaying ties, buy a piece of lattice (either plastic or wood) at the local home improvement store. Plastic is lighter and easier to hang, but wood is more authentic. Using heavy-type glue, affix small pieces of wood to the lattice's back and then mount the lattice to the wall. The wood pieces make the lattice stick out from the wall, making it easier to hang

College of the Canyons Early Childhood Center (Santa Clarita, California)

and display the ties. You can try adhesive strips for damage-free hanging.

Family mobile. Provide wood paint stirrers, and ask children to create a colorful wooden slat to represent their families or selves as part of the classroom community. Drill a hole in the top of each paint stirrer, string them together on a tree branch, and suspend the mobile from the ceiling. When completed, children feel accepted as a part of a larger community in their classroom and at the school. Children felt respected and important when this masterpiece was displayed at a college campus art gallery. The whole community could see the children's beautiful expressions of art.

Wish rocks. Give families the opportunity to express wishes and dreams for their children. Collect stones from the beach, river's edge, or garden shop, and place them in the entryway along with pens for writing messages. Display the wish rocks in a beautiful container such as a wooden tray or apothecary jar. Children are immediately attracted to their parents' wish rocks, and they find joy in handling them.

Hint: Select stones that have smooth surfaces (such as river rocks) and an open area for writing.

United States Air Force Child Development Center (Germany)

Community's Thread

Community culture. New Orleans is known for Mardi Gras and its famous beads. Because beads are so popular in New Orleans, most families have strings of beads tucked away in a closet or junk drawer. Recognizing beads as part of the community's culture, a center capitalized on their popularity. A note asking for bead donations was sent home to the parents, and children brought in a treasure trove of shiny and colorful beads. Children felt important and accepted as they collaborated to make a collage that truly reflects their local community.

Hint: What's important or interesting in your community? Is it jazz music, ethnic food, art galleries, an evergreen forest, a lake, pumpkin patches, the ocean, a skyscraper, an automobile assembly line, grape vineyards, a bowling alley, a historic park, cow pastures, a field museum, a pig farm, a bridge, a symphony orchestra, a flower garden, waterfalls, a railroad station, a button factory, a horse ranch, a steel plant, a tourist attraction, celery flats, a general store, a blueberry festival, beach art, walking trails, the Kentucky Derby, a basket weaver, a corn field, a canyon, a bee farm, a rodeo, a farmer's market, a pottery store, a seaport, windmills, a brick making factory, or the luggage capital of the world? Look around your community with a new perspective—find something interesting, historical, imaginative, and captivating. And figure out how to bring some of these interesting facets of the community into the lives of children in your classroom.

Bellaboo's Children's Play and Discovery Center (Lake Station, Indiana)

City blocks. It is easy to bring the local community into your classroom. You or the children can take photos of their community's buildings including schools, police or fire stations, the library, doctor or dentist offices, animal hospitals, pharmacies, hospitals, and even their own homes. Display the community's images as inspiration for this project. Provide wood pieces and paint, and let the children paint the town! The artisans feel important and included when their neighborhood establishments become a significant part of the classroom.

Hint: Purchase a 2- by 4-inch piece of wood at the local home improvement store. This is a common size of wood, so it should not be difficult to find. You might be able to persuade someone at the store to cut the wood into various lengths, including a few triangle shapes for building roofs. If children use tempera to paint the wood pieces, find time when children are not in the classroom and spray their work with clear acrylic paint to seal the paintings.

The Adventure Club (St. John, Indiana)

By representing and acknowledging the local community and neighborhood in the classroom, you help children understand that they are a part of something bigger than their own home and family. They feel accepted because they share the recognition and knowledge of these landmarks with their classmates. And they feel a connection with the past and present as these common community landmarks are reflected in their everyday play and learning.

Community classroom names. This classroom artwork highlights the cityscape and all the buildings and factories in the area. What do your children know about? What is a famous spot or common area for families to gather? Select a classroom name reflecting your community. It could be based on a neighborhood name near your school or an area of the city or town that has a lake, river, or mountain.

Hint: You could have classroom names reflecting the geographical terrain such as Rocky Mountains, Hudson River, Painted Desert, Grand Canyon, or Niagara Falls. Classrooms could be named after local wildflowers (bluebonnets or violets) or native tree species (birchwood or hickory). Or consider naming classrooms after interesting community monuments or local businesses.

Local treasures. Children who collect artifacts and other local treasures become familiar with the local community's natural world. Displaying local flora and giving opportunities to manipulate and experience these beautiful objects helps children recognize, for example, types and names of plants growing in their neighborhood, community, or region of the country. When they bring these items into the classroom environment to share, they may discover that other children found something similar. With this recognition, children feel accepted as important members of the classroom and community.

Milestones (Charlottetown, Prince Edward Island, Canada)

Chippewa Nature Center's Nature Preschool (Midland, Michigan)

My town. These images from the local community were taken by the teacher and attached to blocks with clear contact paper. When children bring in images from places of interest near their homes and these are mounted on the blocks and placed in the block center, they relate to the images and feel that they are part of a larger group.

Hint: You can use a glue sealer (such as Mod Podge) from the local craft store to attach images to blocks for increased durability.

City blueprints. Check with a local architectural firm to see if they will donate old blueprints to use as a construction base or for wrapping cardboard boxes for city buildings. Children feel important and valued when they receive real-life materials for their projects.

Family blocks. For a weekend project, send white cardboard blocks home for children and parents to create as a family. Do not give them specific directions on what to do with the blocks. Just tell them to have fun, use their creativity, and create a block representative of their family. These family blocks make great additions to the home-living, block, or dramatic-play centers. The blocks can also be used as a strategy for denoting children's arrival into the classroom. When

Chippewa Nature Center's Nature Preschool (Midland, Michigan)

a child comes into the classroom, she can find her family's block and put it in a special place to celebrate her arrival. Children feel included and accepted as they recognize their own family among the collection of family blocks displayed. Children see all the different types of families (blended families, various ethnicities, and extended and single-parent families) living in a community and begin to understand that they are part of a bigger whole.

We Must Begin

It has been said that the environment communicates values. If we are to value children's basic needs, then it is critically important to strengthen the connections

Community Play School (Baltimore, Maryland)

Community Blocks

by Rebecca Kreth

Our idea for creating community blocks came to be one day while observing our young Native children learning about community members. Our curriculum had scripted notes and photos showing people dressed as what is commonly seen as a firefighter, law enforcement officer, or mail delivery person. These commercially purchased images of community helpers did not accurately reflect our children's lives. Children's interest appeared to be distracted when the teacher asked them to identify each community member. Perhaps this was because our Native children have their own community to which they belong (such as tribal health buildings, the school, and offices). These community buildings are all located on ancestral lands, surrounded by the natural beauty of the area, and connected to tribal histories, celebrations, and traditions.

As a teaching team, we decided to photograph the children's beautiful surroundings, including the building structures, mountains, waters, bridges, trains, restaurants, and natural landscapes. We then found woodworkers in the area who donated their block ends from construction of cabinetry and shelving. We collected blocks of all sizes and shapes, and then glued and sealed our photos to the blocks of wood. After we had collected and made approximately twenty blocks for each classroom, we presented the blocks to the children, and they were immediately enthralled. They exclaimed, "That's where my mom works!" "That's my school!" or "That's where I go to the doctor!" Children were able to engage in conversations about their community from a place of knowledge and meaningful experience. These blocks have stayed in the classrooms and continued to engage the children in learning not only about their tribal community but the larger urban community in which they live.

Many children in our classrooms are from a growing number of different cultures; they are looking for connections, seeking to belong, integrating their authentic communities into an understanding of the greater world. As educators of young children, it is important to be mindful of the place and history of all children.

between our classroom and children's families and their communities.

We cannot underestimate the power and influence of our classroom environments on children's growth and development. And we cannot overlook our responsibilities to craft environments reflective of our children, their families, and the communities in which they live. Make the commitment to change. Begin.

Begin by critically evaluating your classroom. Assess the strength of the threads connecting children, families, and communities by answering the questions on the What's Your Classroom Tapestry? questionnaire. Once you have determined its strength, use some of the ideas presented in this chapter to create a beautiful tapestry. Make Bronfenbrenner and Newmark proud!

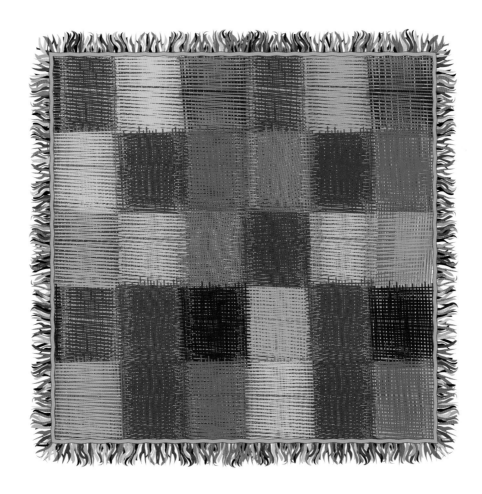

What's Your Classroom Tapestry?

Use this questionnaire to determine if your classroom offers some of the threads (child, family, or community) of Bronfenbrenner's tapestry, and provides opportunities for children to feel respected, included, secure, accepted, and important.

Directions: Select A, B, or C for each item listed below.

A = Strongly agree

B = Agree

C = Strongly disagree

_____ 1. There is space provided near the classroom entryway that includes at least two welcoming features (such as bench or chair, basket of books, framed photographs of families, or table lamp with soft light) giving children and parents a comfortable place to transition from home to school. (Threads: child and family. Basic needs: feel accepted, important, included, and secure)

_____ 2. At least one transitioning activity (such as welcoming stones) helps children transition from home to school. (Threads: child and family. Basic needs: feel accepted, included, and secure)

_____ 3. There is at least one evocative object, provocation, or invitation to engage children that is visible from the classroom entryway, which is specifically designed to help children transition from home to school and to capture their attention and curiosity. (Threads: child and family. Basic needs: feel accepted and included)

_____ 4. There is at least one element or visual image (such as community blocks or cityscapes) reflecting the local community in the classroom. (Threads: child and community. Basic needs: feel accepted and included)

_____ 5. There are at least three locally found, natural elements (such as seashells, pinecones, or tree bark) accessible to children for exploration, which are frequently refreshed and changed. (Threads: child and community. Basic needs: feel included)

_____ 6. There are displays and learning materials specifically designed to honor both teachers' and children's families and uniqueness (Threads:

child, family, and community. Basic Needs: feel respected, important, and accepted)

Scoring:

This tool helps assess the strength of your classroom's tapestry. Remember, the commitment to Bronfenbrenner's tapestry of life and Newmark's basic needs is an ongoing process of learning, so there are no correct answers.

If you responded frequently with an *A*, you are well on your way to a beautiful and strong classroom tapestry meeting the needs of all those connected to your classroom.

If you responded frequently with a *B*, you may have some additional threads to weave into your existing classroom tapestry.

If you responded frequently with a *C*, you may want to consider implementing the ideas in this

chapter to begin weaving the various threads of life into your classroom tapestry.

2

Reenvision Your Classroom Landscape

- -

Beauty is a light in the heart.

—Khalil Gibran, *The Prophet*

An Invitation for Change

If you visited an early childhood classroom in a totally different part of the country from yours, would you know where you are based on what you see? Or would this classroom—located miles and miles away from yours—look pretty much like your own? Would the furniture and equipment (and even its arrangement) look similar? Would the toys and learning materials be identical? Would the rugs and floor covering look pretty much the same? Would the laminated posters and charts be purchased from the same catalogs? Would there be anything unique, any visual clue, any artifact or display to let you know where you might be in the United States? Most probably, there would be no signs to help determine your geographical location because this cookie-cutter classroom looks identical to thousands of other classrooms across the country.

Now consider your own classroom for a moment. Pretend you are seeing your environment for the first time. Would you know where you are based on what you see? Can you see a reflection of those who live, work, and play within the classroom walls? What are the visual signs of the connection between families, their community, and the classroom? Do you see evidence (such as furniture, learning materials, or images) of your classroom's geographical location represented? Or does your classroom look like most other classrooms around the country? Is it a cookie-cutter environment?

This is an invitation to think critically about your classroom's landscape. This is a challenge to look at your environment from a new and perhaps

uncomfortable perspective. This is a call for adjusting your ideas about what constitutes quality environments for young children. This is a summons to break the conventional aesthetic code of classroom design and do away with the traditional notions about early childhood environments. This is an invitation for change.

Aesthetic Code of Preschool Classrooms

When we think of the term *aesthetics*, our minds may have a tendency to gravitate toward the idea of beauty. When thinking about buildings or structures in relationship to aesthetics, our thoughts may lean toward the magnificence of balance, proportion, line, and shape. When considering the aesthetics of a Rembrandt painting, we may look at the splendor of the artwork's texture, color, and light and dark spaces. But aesthetics is more than these physical and observable elements.

Many experts believe aesthetics embraces a social construct. Each person's perception of what is beautiful or aesthetically pleasing is grounded in culture and shaped by social norms. These socially shaped perceptions become expectations that help form our aesthetic codes. Consider, for example, society's accepted expectations when attending an NFL football game. What you don't expect is a quiet, subdued afternoon. You expect crowds of noisy—sometimes overly rambunctious—fans. You anticipate hard (and possibly cold) stadium seats. You look forward to eating a hot dog and smelling popcorn. When you enter the stadium, you look ahead to the half-time show with marching bands and other musical entertainment. You anticipate all this because this is the traditional aesthetic code of an NFL football game. It is our society's socially accepted expectation of what should occur and how it should be.

Early childhood environments also have aesthetic codes. Close your eyes for a moment. Conjure up a traditional preschool classroom in your mind's eye. What do you see? Primary-colored furniture or walls? Area rugs bordered with cartoon figures, shapes, or letters? Brightly colored plastic toys? Shelves stuffed and stacked high with materials? Walls completely covered with children's work or commercially purchased posters depicting every imaginable topic—in both English and Spanish? You envisioned these images because they are traditionally accepted notions of what an early childhood classroom should be. These notions are familiar; they are comfortable. These aesthetic codes have persisted because, until recently, they have not been challenged.

Reconsider Your Classroom Environment

Early childhood experts are beginning to break the traditional ways of thinking about classroom spaces and looking at designing classrooms with new perspectives. Rather than simply filling spaces, the emerging emphasis is on creating meaningful, beautiful, and inspiring environments reflective of those who inhabit the space. Breaking the aesthetic code means buying fewer plastic items and having more natural materials. Rethinking your classroom landscape means using fewer artificial items purchased from a catalog and having more

Chippewa Nature Center's Nature Preschool (Midland, Michigan)

Children's Choice (Prince Albert, Saskatchewan, Canada)

senses—think about the sight of fiery sunsets and gorgeous mountain peaks, the delicious smells of home-baked cinnamon buns and newly mowed grass, the feel of a newborn's velvety face and warm summer sun on our skin, the sounds of birds welcoming the morning and cool crisp water in a gurgling stream . . . and the tangy tastes of barbeque shrimp and homemade lemonade. Beauty, however, is much more than sensorial pleasure. Beauty is an emotion. When we experience something beautiful with our senses, we also experience this beauty through our emotions. Gardner asserted that without emotions, learning cannot happen.

real-world, authentic objects. It means stocking fewer commercially purchased toys and providing more recycled, found, and loose parts. Acquiring a new perspective means reducing the number of institutional or commonplace objects and choosing more beautiful and evocative objects instead.

More Beauty, Less Institution

Beauty is powerful. As educator Howard Gardner noted in his book *Truth, Beauty, and Goodness Reframed*, it is a basic human need that shapes and defines our very essence. Beauty gives pleasure to our minds and our

Frequent encounters with elements of beauty help humans become all they can be. Children are no exception when it comes to needing beauty in their lives. Because children spend countless hours in a child care environment, it is vitally important for early childhood practitioners to eliminate the cold and institutional elements of the classroom and infuse an infinite amount of beauty for all to enjoy. When children experience beauty, they also experience a sense of awe and curiosity. Beautiful objects magnetize children's attention and solicit their observations to the properties of the objects.

> If we furnish our houses and schools with only indestructible, childproof, throwaway, and discardable objects; it teaches children to be careless in the use of things. On the other hand, if they use beautiful objects and something of value is damaged, a teachable moment occurs. Grief is expressed and real values are learned. Children learn about caring.
> —**Marvin Bartel**, "Art in Everyday Life"

Inspiring spaces are places of beauty. Beauty promotes wonder. Wonder instills lifelong learning.

Cognition and emotions are closely linked, and beauty stimulates emotions. This experience can be referred to as *a sense of wonder*, which involves instinctually noticing and responding to what is beautiful and awe-inspiring. Much more pronounced in children than in adults, the sense of wonder can be seen in the way children respond to and interact with certain elements of nature. And, as educator Ruth Wilson notes in *Learning Is in Bloom*, wonder promotes children's knowledge of the world in which they live. Whether you provide opportunities to experience beauty through provocative classroom objects, encourage and provide tools for creating art in a variety of mediums, or infuse

the joy of music and dance into children's activities, you can infuse a sense of wonder in their lives. Beautiful classrooms are inspiring and powerful, and have a lasting effect on young children.

Many classrooms tend to be institutional, as Jim Greenman notes in his article "Places for Childhoods: How Institutional Are You?" Uniformity and rules are the primary values of institutions, he asserts, which control and dehumanize all those who reside

and play within the walls. In an attempt to meet ever-tightening health, education, and environmental standards, classrooms have lost their individuality and are becoming increasingly sterile and uniform. When designing early childhood environments, educators often focus on the classroom's functionality for children to operate as a whole within a group setting. Although teachers give much thought to the arrangement of the equipment and furniture as well as the number and type of learning materials, they often overlook the idea of creating beautiful environments.

It is time to bring beauty to the children. It is time to surround children with beauty in the classroom by adding the natural elements of light and sound; providing books with photographs and realistic illustrations; offering objects of provocation and wonder; including pottery, sculptures, gallery-worthy works of art, and mobiles; and infusing nature and natural elements into the classroom. Equally important is offering children opportunities to create beauty.

Using varied shapes and sizes of bottles, children created beautiful décor for the window's ledge. Adding some liquid glue to tempera paint helps the paint adhere to the glass bottles. Many early childhood educators believe the benefits of including glass in the classroom outweigh the possible risks. Some educators use mason jars for

United States Air Force Child Development Center (Japan)

storing loose parts, offer porcelain coffee cups in the home-living area, and place decorative glass objects throughout the classroom.

Art canvases make the perfect backdrop for children's artwork. Children first covered the canvas with liquid glue and then pressed peppercorns in the glue. After the glue dried, children painted the entire canvas with black tempera mixed with liquid glue and then

Board of Jewish Education Early Childhood Center at Beth Hillel (Wilmette, Illinois)

Rethinking the Classroom Landscape

dropped some more pink peppercorns to finish off their masterpiece.

With a found wicker seat, children wove natural materials to create a beautiful landscape of texture and natural colors.

Hope's Home
(Prince Albert, Saskatchewan, Canada)

Just for You (Charlottetown, Prince Edward, Canada)

Children's Choice (Prince Albert, Saskatchewan, Canada)

Children added natural elements such as twigs and wheat to a piece of bark found in their local community. Notice the metal washers and bolts in the middle of the image.

Using a paint mixture of liquid glue and tempera paint, children decorated large tree cookies to make a brilliant display for the classroom's windowsill.

Children's Home + Aid (Carpentersville, Illinois)

Rethinking the Classroom Landscape

Milestones Early Childhood Development Center (Stratford, Prince Edward Island, Canada)

To make a beaded curtain, children can string beads on fanciful and different colored ribbons, which then hang from a bamboo rod. This makes a gorgeous backdrop for a quiet or dramatic-play area.

Colorful weaving projects hung around the classroom can promote creativity and recognize children's artistic contributions.

To create a nature bracelet, position duct tape sticky side out as a bracelet on the child's wrist. Take a nature hike, and let children collect and press natural objects on the bracelet. Once back to the classroom, display the bracelets in a prominent place.

Children arranged pony beads in a single layer with the pattern of their choice in a non-stick pan to create a sun catcher. You can melt the beads in a 350-degree oven for 20 to 30 minutes. Of course, children should not be near the heated beads. Once the design is cool, the sun catcher can easily be popped out of the pan. Hang it in a window with a suction cup hook. Hint: When children arrange pony beads in the pan, you can suggest that they purposefully leave a hole or space to be used later for a string to hang the sun catcher.

Milgard Child Development Center at Pierce College (Lakewood, Washington)

Beauty can be made from most anything—in this case, children used donated metal objects such as nuts, bolts, washers, curtain hangers, and wheels from a discarded toy truck to create a glowing figure.

After thinly sliced citrus fruits have been dried in the oven, children thread the fruits onto nylon fishing line. This scented mobile of dried fruit looks delicious in the classroom, especially hanging in the home-living center. Citrus fruits include grapefruit, oranges, limes, and lemons.

The Adventure Club (Munster, Indiana)

Children's Place (Tampa, Florida)

Note: To extend the fruity scent, spray the mobile with citrus-smelling room freshener. Be sure to consider the age of children and any potential choking hazards when choosing loose parts for play and creative activities.

Children are beautiful miracles, and they deserve to be surrounded by beauty in their lives. Their bodies, minds, and spirits are ever-open to wonder and imagination. It is our responsibility to enfold children with interesting and wondrous materials to examine,

manipulate, and explore. It is our responsibility to shape environments into aesthetically beautiful places where children can learn and grow. In addition to child-made beauty, another way to infuse beauty in the classroom is by taking and displaying images of the children engaging in their work.

Also, be on the lookout for beautiful objects to photograph. Although traditional cameras are a good way to

capture beauty, you can also use your cell phone if it has picture-taking capabilities. You can then download the photo and print it out on glossy photograph paper. Or send your electronic image to a company that specializes in affixing your image to a canvas backing.

More Natural, Less Plastic

Many children today are growing up with the feel of asphalt and the smell of plastic. Plastic is all around us. It is so commonplace in our stores, classrooms, and homes that for many of us, the idea of plastic emitting a smell is a foreign thought. Regardless, the smell is there. Have you ever purchased a vinyl shower curtain for your home and noticed the smell when you open the packaging? You might breathe in the plastic odor and think "Ahhh . . . it smells new." What you really smell are chemicals used in processing this man-made product, which the Center for Health, Environment and Justice (http://chej.org/) notes could possibly be harmful to your health.

In addition to the chemical odor, plastic is also visually and kinesthetically uninteresting because it has minimal depth and little texture. Consider, for example, the difference between a plastic tea set and an authentic silver teapot. Most plastic teapots look and feel pretty much the same. Their smooth surfaces

The Smell of Plastic

----

by Sandra Duncan

While reading *Last Child in the Woods*, I came across Richard Louv's assertion that today's children are growing up on the smell of plastic. My thoughts were, "What? Really? I don't think so. Plastic doesn't have a smell." And my narrow-minded thinking remained steadfast until I entered a four-story dollar (100 yen) store in Japan.

Whatever you wanted or needed, you could get in this gigantic store. It was stuffed and overstuffed. The amount of stuff—mostly plastic—from floor to ceiling was astounding. The aisles were so narrow you could hardly push a small cart through. There was no room for passing side by side in the aisles because of the overabundance of merchandise.

When I first opened the door to enter this store, my nose was overwhelmed by an unusual smell. "Goodness me! What's that smell?" I wondered. Guess what? It was the smell of plastic! Louv was right: Plastic does have an odor, and it's not that pleasant.

have few nooks and crannies for children's eyes and hands to explore. An authentic silver teapot with its many and varied bumps and textures, on the other hand, not only is more visually and kinesthetically appealing but also serves the purpose of fostering a connection to the real world.

Plastic is also uninspiring. Made of synthetic materials, it adds little or no beauty to the early childhood classroom. Yet plastic is so ingrained in our everyday lives and early childhood classrooms that it is hard to imagine life without it. Most cookie-cutter classrooms have a lot of plastic: toys, games, manipulatives, blocks,

chairs, tables, painting easels, teddy bear counters, pretend food, baskets, trucks, blocks, and the list goes on and on. Take an inventory of the plastic furniture, equipment, toys, and learning materials in your classroom. How much plastic do you have?

What's Your Plastic Inventory?

Directions: Count the number of plastic items in each category and record the number in the last column. If you have items that do not fit in a category, note them under Other.

Category	How Many Plastic Items?
Tables and chairs	
Shelves	
Toys and Games	
Blocks	
Manipulatives counters	
Musical instruments	
Play equipment (such as a sand table or play house)	
Art tools	
Large-muscle equipment (such as slides)	
Baskets, containers, and bins	
Dramatic-play materials (such as dishes)	
Other	

Were you surprised at the amount of plastic in your room? Do you think the amount of plastic outweighs other types of materials such as steel, wood, glass, or natural materials?

To find out the answer to this question, stand in the middle of your classroom and slowly turn around in a circle. As you are turning, note the types of materials in your classroom. Do you see more plastic than wood or other natural materials? If so, think about swapping out plastic items for natural elements. Use wood tables rather than plastic. If you are unable to replace the plastic table, cover it with a piece of muslin or find a tree stump to use for a table. In place of brightly colored plastic baskets, use wicker baskets or wood bowls. Instead of plastic teddy bear counters for math manipulatives, use objects from nature such as rocks, lentils, pebbles, or buckeyes.

Instead of purchasing games from the toy store, consider making your own learning materials and manipulatives using natural elements such as pine-cones or rocks. Instead of using plastic rolling pins for clay play, use corn cobs. To get you started swapping out plastic for natural materials, think about the ideas that follow.

Use Natural and Unique Containers

Containers in the early childhood classroom are so commonplace that we rarely give them a second thought.

Yet containers are essential for children's activities. Think about all the containers in your classroom. Most likely, you have a variety of sizes and shapes of baskets and bins sitting on your shelves. Most of these containers are probably made from plastic. Consider swapping out all or some of your plastic baskets for natural containers. You can find interesting and unique containers to hold children's materials at garage sales or resale shops when you embrace the mind-set of needing a vessel for classroom objects and not just looking for a traditional plastic basket.

Old-fashioned wooden plant containers provide a perfect place to keep children's art tools such as markers, scissors, pencils, and crayons.

Keep an eye out for wooden bowls at estate sales or farmhouse yard sales. Not only are wood bowls durable, they are visually interesting because of the various knotholes and wood grains.

Visit the local antique store to see if you can find solid-wood containers at a reasonable price. Sometimes you get lucky and find a truly unique container to hold classroom materials.

Child-made containers promote feelings of ownership and a sense of pride. Children often will transform an ordinary cardboard box into an extraordinary container.

Metal candy dishes or wooden or wicker bowls from recycled-goods stores make great containers for natural materials. The tiered metal dishes pictured above can fold up for storage when not in use.

In the art area, bricks make convenient organizers for tools such as paper hole punchers and scissors.

Rethinking the Classroom Landscape

It's easy to make a container like this one. Find a small log and simply drill as many holes as you need to hold crayons, markers, or pencils.

Small ceramic bowls and spoons provide wonderful containers for science experiments.

Replace Plastic Art Tools with Natural Tools
Early childhood classrooms typically use art tools purchased from a catalog or at the local store. Many of these commercially purchased art tools are manufactured from plastic. Art tools made from nature, on the other hand, have the earth's power and are truly authentic. Nature art tools also inspire more open-ended artistic explorations.

Rethinking the Classroom Landscape

With a plastic-handled paint brush, for instance, children tend to singularly apply paint on the paper. With paintbrushes made from sticks, flowers, and pine boughs, which are bound together with rubber bands, children's creativity and imaginations are sparked! Try putting away the traditional art tools made of plastic such as plastic brushes, stencils, and rollers, and replacing them with art tools from nature.

For painting, other paintbrush options include reeds and grasses, bundled leaves, willow branches, cattails, wheat stalks, feathers, sea or natural sponges, seaweed, or tree pods. Natural elements that can work as rolling pins include round rocks, tree twigs, bamboo sticks, gourds, and tree cookies.

The Plastic Bag Replacement Project

by Jay Sinha, activist for a plastic-free planet

A few years ago in our community of Wakefield, Quebec, our local fair trade committee decided to tackle the problem of plastic-bag pollution and overuse. We created an awareness campaign and asked local retailers to help spread the word and offer reusable bags. We did a presentation about the problem of plastic bags at the local elementary school on Earth Day. The presentation talked about the roughly five trillion plastic bags produced each year and how they are made from earth-scarring fossil fuels such as oil and natural gas, with plasticizing chemicals added. Then they are shipped across the world, often to be used for a few minutes before being discarded, sometimes directly into the environment where they pollute, block drainage systems, and kill wildlife.

The children were then invited to come up with suggestions to assist with the community campaign, and to draw posters with messages on them. They came up with suggestions such as bring your own bag, use a reusable bag, keep bags in your car, use cloth bags, use reusable lunch bags, compost so you have less garbage, tell people not to litter, use boxes for groceries, pick up any plastic bags you see on the ground, and reuse your plastic bags.

The posters they created were put up around the community and in stores to help get the message out.

My favorite poster showed the planet Earth in space with other planets in the distance. Floating plastic bags surrounded Earth. Written on our planet was the question: Do you want this?

So here's a suggestion: Identify one plastic item in your classroom and engage the children in a project to replace it with an alternative. For example, the class could replace plastic building blocks with cut and sanded trunk rounds from small fallen trees. The children could gather the trunks from a nearby forest, then parents or a woodworker could prepare them. Or—better yet—the children themselves could prepare the tree rounds. It's important that the children know why they are replacing plastic with natural materials. That knowledge will filter over to their friends, siblings, and parents, creating waves of change.

In her book *The Sense of Wonder*, Rachel Carson explains that when introducing a child to the natural world, "It is not half so important to know as to feel." Imagine the wonder that could be inspired if classroom environments actually did mimic the natural world by including only natural materials. Let's help our children understand that the feel of plastic is not natural.

You can get more ideas on the Life Without Plastic website (www.lifewithoutplastic.com).

The Nature Preschool at Irvine Nature Center (Owings Mills, Maryland)

Swap Plastic for Natural and Unique Manipulatives

In place of plastic game counters, teddy bears, or math manipulatives, use natural objects such as rocks, seashells, acorns, or buckeyes. Not only are natural materials more visually and texturally appealing to young children, they can foster a connection to the natural world. The more time children spend with natural items, the more these children prefer them over plastic and other commercially purchased objects.

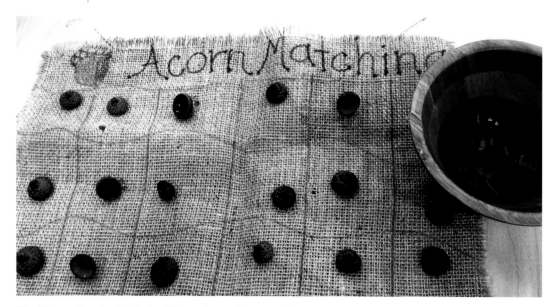

The Nature Preschool at Irvine Nature Center (Owings Mills, Maryland)

The Nature Preschool at Irvine Nature Center (Owings Mills, Maryland)

The Nature Preschool at Irvine Nature Center (Owings Mills, Maryland)

Perhaps it is the feel of the smooth Oregon river rock, the texture of the Texas gigantic acorn, the soft and worn bumps on the Michigan driftwood, or the smell of Indiana's fresh rosemary. Regardless of what draws and magnetizes children to nature, it is important to infuse your classroom with natural and sensory-rich objects.

Child Development and Learning Laboratory at Central Michigan University (Mount Pleasant, Michigan)

Rethinking the Classroom Landscape

Incorporate Natural Equipment and Furniture

One way to reduce plastic in the indoor and outdoor environment is to use tree stumps for chairs, tables, and other apparatus or classroom equipment. Tree stumps come in all sizes and shapes. And they are easy to obtain. After a storm, for example, find someone who is chopping up a fallen tree and ask if you can have the pieces. Most of the time, they are even willing to load the stumps or logs into your vehicle. If you are concerned about bugs or insects, simply spray the

stumps with bleach water several times and leave out in hot sun. Or cover with a thin coat of clear shellac.

Although this balance beam is outside, it could easily be brought into the classroom. Made out of a tree stump and logs, the beam not only is practical but can be made from a fallen tree—which is free of charge. The only hard part to this project is finding someone who will help cut the notches in the stump.

Chippewa Nature Center's Nature Preschool (Midland, Michigan)

A Challenge

- - - - - - - -

by Rachel A. Larimore, director of education, Chippewa Nature Center's Nature Preschool

Nature-based preschools do not have to be at nature centers! It's my dream that every preschool in the country would be nature-based. After all, it is nature that helps define place. By connecting to nature, we're creating a sense of place for our children, making learning relevant and meaningful, and building the ultimate connection between school and home because both are encompassed by this greater concept called "place." The natural world is with us everywhere and at every moment—even in the most urban areas.

Natural elements define our place, determine the landmarks where we play, and even inspire the community festivals we celebrate. The stars we see at night are unique to our place in time and space. The trees and herbaceous plants are unique to our region of the world. Natural bodies of water in your place may have salt or not, or they may be a special treat after a rare rainfall.

I challenge all early childhood educators to find natural elements unique to their place in the world. Imagine a world where all children grow up having a strong understanding for the natural elements that influence the sights, sounds, and smells of their community. Now, even more amazing is a world where those children also understand how those natural elements support our social relationships and interactions, including our economy. It starts by integrating nature into every preschool classroom in the country. Again, I challenge every early childhood educator to begin integrating nature into their indoor space, bring natural loose parts into their play areas, and venture outside the fence to explore the natural world. Nature is everywhere!

Find Unique Uses for Plastic

Because plastic is everywhere, completely eliminating it from the classroom is an unrealistic expectation. So begin considering some unique uses for plastic and thereby keeping plastic from your community's landfill.

Image courtesy of Community Playthings

More Loose Parts, Fewer Toys

The theory of loose parts was first proposed back in the 1970s by architect Simon Nicholson, who believed that loose parts in the environment can empower children's creativity. Loose parts are materials that can be moved, carried, combined, lined up, redesigned, and put back together in all sorts of different ways. Typically, these materials do not have any specific directions and can be used alone or in combination with other materials.

There are many types of loose parts such as synthetic manufactured items, natural, or recycled objects. Examples of natural loose parts include rocks, twigs, dried corn, seashells, pine cones, driftwood, seeds, leaves, and vines. Buttons, bottle caps, cardboard tubes, polyvinyl chloride (PVC) pipes, yarn, wire, mosaic tiles, sea glass, and fabric are examples of manufactured or recycled loose parts. Of course, you will want to consider safety and avoid choking hazards; choose loose parts that are appropriate for the children's developmental levels. The advantage of loose parts is that children can use them as a springboard for play.

Refresh Loose Parts

With the addition of some interesting loose parts (such as nuts and bolts, and PVC piping), the typical block center might get turned into a space ship, train, or hotel by children using their imaginations, the blocks, and new and interesting loose parts. In a Canadian

Nancy W. Darden Child Development Center at East Carolina University (Greenville, North Carolina)

preschool classroom, the hubcaps, tire rims, and other metal items became a Ferris wheel (with a vertical orientation) until the child saw a scrambler ride (with a horizontal orientation) at the community fairgrounds

Photo courtesy of Mickey MacGillivray, Hope's Home (Prince Albert, Saskatchewan, Canada)

66

and changed his creation. A child's perspective and knowledge about her world continually changes and is in constant flux based on what she experiences and observes, so it is important to refresh the loose parts on a frequent basis.

Keep Loose Parts Visible

In addition to fostering creativity, using loose parts allows children to be messy and do real and meaningful work as they construct and move the objects around to compose their stories. Loose parts are also developmentally appropriate because children interact with them in ways to suit their own developmental levels. Children at different ages use the same loose parts differently. A three-year-old might line up rocks as a boundary around a block structure, and yet a four-year-old may actually incorporate the rocks into the structure.

Children display an infinite amount of creativity when using these open-ended materials. Their discoveries are only limited by the number of loose parts provided to them. But it is important to keep loose parts visible for inspiration.

There is truth to the old adage: "Out of sight, out of mind." According to some creativity experts, people get inspired by what is around them. So it is with children. Provide children with inspiration and keep loose parts in their immediate line of sight.

Showcasing loose materials "accelerates the potential for those magical moments of creative inspiration," as Scott Doorley and Scott Witthoft noted in their book *Make Space: How to Set the Stage for Creative Collaboration.*

Create Classroom Metal Centers

Metal is an ideal loose part. Metal objects have an authentic feel and come in a variety of sizes, types, and forms. Metal objects are easily obtainable and second-hand items are usually inexpensive. Children often find metal items irresistible for exploration and open-ended play. Metal loose parts fit seamlessly into many areas of the classroom. For example, including nuts and bolts in the art, block, and dramatic-play centers can provide children valuable opportunities for construction and creative play.

One of the easiest ways to include metal as a loose part is in the block center. Although the block center is a popular area in the early childhood classroom, it sometimes becomes static because the materials within the center rarely change. A typical block center includes unit blocks, transportation signs (such as stop or railroad signs), people figurines, wooden trees, and perhaps plastic dinosaurs or farm animals.

Infusing the uniqueness of metal as a loose part opens up a world of endless possibilities, opportunities, and construction challenges. Here are some ideas to get you started:

- Wire baskets
- Pans and lids
- Keys
- Pie tins
- Colanders
- Juice-jar lids
- Pieces of wire
- Jewelry
- Screens
- Kitchen utensils
- Locks
- Whisks
- Canning lids and rings
- Hubcaps
- Bicycle wheel

- Springs
- Short chains
- Nuts and bolts
- Funnels and scoops
- Tin boxes
- Paper clips
- Wire baskets
- Door knobs
- Colanders
- Egg beater
- Cooling racks

Note: Be aware of safety considerations and use only objects appropriate for the age group you teach.

If you really want to change the landscape of your classroom, include a metal corner. Treat it like any of your other learning areas in the classroom. Just like the block center and dramatic-play area, it is always there, always open, always accessible to children. It can be a large center or just a small spot in the classroom. Regardless of the size, just watch how the children's creativity and excitement blossom!

Metal centers can be as small as what fits on a wicker place mat or in a small basket, or they can include an assortment of large items that fill up a big area outside. Consider making a ring-and-ping metal-instrument center. Look around the kitchen for unwanted or unused utensils, pots, pans, muffin tins, baking trays, and lids. You might want to distribute a note to parents asking if they have any old metal kitchen objects. Also, scrounge garage sales or visit resale shops for inexpensive objects. Then you can hang all the found objects on a fence. Children can use metal whisks, paintbrushes, or rubber-ended hammers for making music on pots, pans, and baking tins. Because little or no money is invested, simply recycle the banged-up instruments or possibly repaint them.

Photo courtesy of Mickey MacGillivray, Hope's Home (Prince Albert, Saskatchewan, Canada)

Country Child Care (Moody, Texas)

More Recycled Materials, Fewer New Items

If you are looking for ways to save money, you can transform unwanted objects and pieces of furniture into creative additions for your classroom. All it takes is a little ingenuity and perhaps a coat of paint. Sometimes it only takes repositioning the object and inventing a new purpose for it.

You can find interesting and authentic furniture at a resale shop or flea market. Think about how you could use a piece of furniture for something other than its original intentions or design.

The Saul Spielberg Early Childhood Center (St. Louis, Missouri)

The Saul Spielberg Early Childhood Center (St. Louis, Missouri)

Board of Jewish Education Early Childhood Center at Beth Hillel (Winnetka, Illinois)

Consider repositioning or rethinking classroom furniture. You can turn a traditional piece of equipment upside down or on its side to transform its use.

Try looking for an old-fashioned round kitchen table. Sometimes you can find these priceless pieces of furniture at farm auction or estate sales. They are well constructed and made of durable and hard wood. You can cut the table pedestal to fit a child's height, place it in the home-living area, and watch children's dramatic play come to life with this authentic piece of furniture.

When you think creatively, you can find a new function for an item of furniture. For example, an old wine rack could be used to hold assorted loose parts. Or you could apply a fresh coat of paint on an old chest of drawers from a resale shop and place it in the home-living area for storage of dress-up clothes.

Discovery Early Learning Center (Poolesville, Maryland)

Piper Center for Family Studies and Child Development at Baylor University (Waco, Texas)

Nelson Street Head Start with Region 16 (Amarillo, Texas)

What Are Your Classroom Aesthetics?

Use the checklist below to evaluate whether the emphasis in your classroom is on creating a meaningful, beautiful, and inspiring environment reflective of those who inhabit the space or a more institutional cookie-cutter classroom space.

Directions: Select *A*, *B*, or *C* for each item listed below.

A = Strongly Agree

B = Agree

C = Strongly Disagree

_____ 1. There are at least two objects of beauty, wonder, or provocation (such as a large seashell, a honeycomb, or prisms) in the classroom.

_____ 2. In addition to children's artwork being displayed, there are images of natural elements (such as trees, flowers, or waterscapes) present in the classroom.

_____ 3. There are more baskets made from natural materials than from plastic.

_____ 4. At least five authentic items are placed in the dramatic-play center (such as a silver teapot, stainless steel serving utensils, a small china tea set, cloth napkins, or place mats).

_____ 5. There is a place in the classroom to play with metal objects.

_____ 6. At least two pieces of equipment, furniture, or furnishings in the classroom are from natural materials (such a tree stump used as a table or chair).

_____ 7. At least two artifacts of child-made beauty are displayed in the classroom.

_____ 8. Several framed photographs of children engaged in meaningful work are displayed in the classroom.

_____ 9. There is a designated area where children can construct with loose parts.

Scoring:

This tool helps assess the commitment to creating an environment that is beautifully aesthetic, meaningful, and inspiring. Remember that the commitment to these dispositions is an ongoing process of learning, so there are no correct answers.

If you responded frequently with the answer *A*, you are well on your way to a beautiful, meaningful, and inspiring classroom environment.

If you responded frequently with a *B*, you may have some additional items to add to your classroom or to remove in order to make it more aesthetically appealing to children.

If you responded frequently with a *C*, you may want to consider implementing some of the ideas in this chapter and begin to include the various elements suggested in this chapter to create a more aesthetically beautiful environment.

3

Transforming Spaces into Places

The catalyst that converts any physical location—any environment if you will—into a place, is the process of experiencing deeply. A place is a piece of the whole environment that has been claimed by feelings…. We are homesick for places.

—Alan Gussow, *A Sense of Place*

A Sense of Place

Places shape us. They influence our moods, behaviors, and our way of thinking and believing. Places dictate how we act, the clothing we wear, and even what we say. They influence what we will or will not become. Places shape human history and the stories of our lives. Naturalist, historian, and educator Ralph Lutts called these life chronicles *ecological conversations*. He noted that these interactions hinge on the physical space and ongoing dialogues between ourselves and the places in which we gather to learn and love. Collectively and individually, we shape our dwellings through meaningful conversations influenced by our own cultural perceptions and unique ideas about the places we live. We reconfigure and align the places based on our personal notions of how the environment should

A Childhood Place—Rich with Nature

by John Rosenow, founder, Arbor Day Foundation

My childhood was rich with nature.

I remember how it tasted and smelled, how it felt to the touch, and the emotions that it evoked.

Nature was right outside the door of our farm home. I knew the location of every fruit source, domestic and wild, and when each fruit ripened: blackberries and raspberries, wild plums and sour cherries, apricots and peaches, and apples.

Our fruit trees were pesticide free, and eating the apples offered lessons of their own: You learned to first take a small bite of each apple, and look at the apple before chewing or swallowing. If you saw half of a worm on the apple you were holding, you spit out the bite and chewed elsewhere. If no worm was in evidence, it was safe to chew.

The mulberry trees were special favorites, growing in the windbreak by our home. We had a purple-stained sheet, which was washed regularly, but kept for placing under the trees when the mulberries were ripe and ready to fall if the fruit-laden branches were shaken. They were sweet goodness eaten one by one or on cereal.

A mulberry tree even contributed modestly to my early intellectual development. At my request, my dad nailed a couple of wide boards onto a large, low-growing horizontal branch, making a little seat and back rest that served as a child-size retreat for reading my favorite books. I savored the comfort of my private little tree-house study for hours on end.

A little boy soon learns the best places to dig in the dirt. I knew where the soil had too much clay and was hard to dig, and where it was black and malleable, and easy to scoop and pile and shape.

I even learned the subtle differences between the smells of a ripe corn or milo field or even a wheat field. And I recall the absolute marvel of standing at the edge of a field of ripe wheat with its golden-yellow heads waving gently in the breeze as far as the eye can see.

Playing in nature offered countless opportunities for many kinds of learning, especially creative problem solving such as figuring out how to maneuver in the fruit bushes to get the berries and avoid the thorns, how to build complex structures with sticks and mud and other found objects, how to find your way back to the house from within a field of tall corn, how to safely climb the tree when the best fruit was toward the top. And playing in nature taught me the necessity of patience. No matter how much I wanted it otherwise, the fruit is not ripe until it's ripe.

look and feel. In many respects, we reshape our places to fit our preconceptions. For someone who lives near the ocean, a preconceived notion of home decorating might include driftwood, sea glass, and seashells. Someone living on the fiftieth floor of a New York City skyscraper might rule out using grandma's furniture or country kitchen curtains on the inoperable steel windows. When furnishing early childhood classrooms, however, there is a tendency to rely on traditionally accepted notions or commercially rendered images instead of environments reflective of the children and the local community. Designing and equipping a reflective classroom goes beyond supplying certain learning materials, providing the furniture and equipment, and arranging and organizing the contents of the room. The ideal, connected approach is not to simply fill classroom spaces. Rather, it is to create an environment with feeling. It is to design a beautiful, respectful environment that is meaningful to children. By engaging in valuable ecological conversations, we can create a place.

Distinction between Space and Place

Space and *place* are commonly used words denoting common experiences, although at times these words often describe very different experiences:

- There's no place like home.
- Hawaii's beaches are gorgeous spaces.
- Grandma's place smells like cinnamon.

- There is a cozy space in the corner of the classroom where children curl up and read.
- The graveyard is a spooky place at night.

In addition to these words being used as descriptors, all types of professions and occupations are involved in the concepts of space and place. Architects design space. Geographers study places. Oceanographers explore deep-water spaces. Astronauts fly into outer space. Housekeepers clean home and office spaces. City planners create community spaces. Explorers find unchartered places. Geologists dig in spaces of dirt. Cowboys might feel out of place at a black-tie affair. Home decorators design fashionable spaces.

Spaces and places are the fundamental components of the world in which we live. Being asked, then, to think about the difference between space and place might at first seem simplistic and unimportant. The concept of place, however, is quite complex. It not only encompasses emotional relationships but also involves experiential perspectives such as smelling, touching, tasting, hearing, and seeing. A sense of place recognizes the importance of neighborhood and community; promotes the connection between past and present with the people who live in the community; acknowledges the influences of geography, topography, flora, and fauna; and understands the importance of human relationships.

Space

A space is an area with no emotional connection. It could be an area surrounded by walls or barriers, and perhaps it includes doors and windows. It could be an open area in an otherwise thick forest. A space could be the spot where you stand while waiting in line for an amusement park ride. The bus seat on which you sit every morning on your way to work could be a space. The gap in highway traffic could be a space for your car to squeeze into. The tape line on which children must mutely stand to go outside could be a space. Spaces have little social connection and few emotional relationships, and minimal meaning or importance is attached to them.

Place

A place is an area with emotional relationships and personal interactions. It is an area where people form attachments to home and community. A space becomes a place when human emotions and relationships are vigorous. In *A Sense of Place: The Artist and the American Land,* artist Alan Gussow notes that people are homesick for places where they can feel and experience deeply. For example, a newly married couple's home is just a space with outer walls, doors, and windows. It becomes a place when the partners add personal artifacts and

Image courtesy of Community Playthings

furniture, and when they celebrate their first anniversary or bring their newborn home. The objects and places within the home become centers of value because of sensory and emotional connections, which become long-term attachments and memories. The partners have had deep experiences and have bonded with their home. They have created a place.

There's a Place for Us

by Courtney Gardner, director of Community Play School

We closed our place today. We're moving to a new spot, and although it's a bit overwhelming, it's also pretty thrilling. We've swept up and leaned the broom against the wall. It's time to move on. It's just an empty space now.

I think it's safe to say that we are all very excited about the change and looking forward to being in our new building. Our old place grew slowly with the program over the years. I'd say it happened pretty organically. We learned a lot, together in that space. We created a community there.

We learned how to be together and how to use every nook and cranny of our available space. The halls became our Main Street and the doorways our stoops. We (the teachers) made a decision to look out for each other and our classes as we used the entire space . . . much like families in a neighborhood work in the yard or on the porch while the children play up and down the block. There is a freedom in knowing your boundaries and exploring every inch of your available space. Children were given the opportunity to explore beyond their classroom doors, and the adults shouldered the burden of keeping track, maintaining ratios, and supervising all of that wonderful activity.

We also learned to trust each other and we began to focus much of our energy on building relationships with individual children and the groups they formed. We learned to adapt the environment to the needs of the children and we learned how to manage all of those loose parts. In many ways, these lessons seem deeply connected to that specific building. I think we are all feeling a bit uncertain about how those lessons will apply in our new school. It's exciting to think about what the new building might teach us.

As I consider all the work ahead, I believe we're less interested in creating an environment that will teach children what they might need to know and more interested in creating a place where we can reveal ourselves. I hope we will create an environment that fosters relationships, supports our values, and makes children and adults feel that they belong and have a voice in their day-to-day lives and especially at school.

(continues)

Now it's time to think about how our new physical environment might foster those values. We're painting the walls and furniture and trying to make the rooms feel welcoming. We want the colors to sit somewhere between a blank canvas and an exciting invitation to play. We're making sure there's space and some places to move our bodies. We'll need to sit down once in a while and we might like to climb or swing. It's also important to create quiet spaces and places to be alone or with the only person we might feel like being with. We're considering all of these ideas as we put the classrooms together.

Most of us like to go outside from time to time. Sometimes we like to go out for long stretches of time, and sometimes we just need a quick blast of fresh air. We need to dig and climb and build. I think we like to do most of the things we enjoy inside even more when we're outside. Outside also allows for bigger projects, less cleaning up, and lots and lots of water. We need to be sure to provide all of these things. It can be difficult to find the balance between preparing our space for the children we already know and wondering who they might become over the course of the coming school year.

As for the materials—those things beyond furniture and carpets—we'll consider the things we've loved in the past, and we'll make a few predictions about where those interests might lead. This gets tricky as we make our plans and think about the children who will fill these rooms in September.

We've made sure to bring along some of our favorite things. We moved the clay table to the new school. We're considering adding at least one more of those because it's very popular and satisfies so many needs for a variety of children. We brought the easels and paint and paper and brushes and many, many other tools for making art. We brought light tables and water tables and, of course, we brought the mats. All of the mats will find a home in our new building. I honestly feel that the mats are one of the most important parts of the old school and they will continue to play a very important role in the new school. I hope (think, believe) the mats tell children that it is absolutely ok to be who they are, to trust their impulses, and to feel their power. The mats say a lot about who we are and what we value as a school community.

For now, we're focusing on creating a place that offers time, space, and freedom. In a few weeks, the children will arrive and our space will become a place and we will begin to fill the rooms with our personalities, interests, and relationships.

An everyday view from an Alaskan kitchen window: Children can see images of birchwood trees, moose, and snow.

Concept of Classroom Space and Reality of Place

Most of a child's life is spent in classrooms. Aside from sleeping and perhaps playing, no other activity occupies a child's time more than attending school. Children have few breaks during the school day when they are able to escape the four walls of the classroom. Although junior high and high school students can move around to different classrooms during the day, preschool children tend to do less of that. It is important, therefore, to understand how to create the sense of place in a young child's environment.

Classroom as a Space

The physical structure of most classrooms is similar. Typically, we have walls acting as the area's boundaries and doors leading to a common hallway, another classroom, or outside. Most classrooms have several windows, and some are fortunate enough to have skylights. Some have bathrooms located within the classroom, and others have a source of water for food preparation or art activities. Classrooms may have built-in storage areas or children's cubbies. The floors may be tile, carpet, or wood. Some classrooms have pillars, archways, or other interesting shapes. Regardless of the kinds and types of physical structures and its contents, a classroom is just a space without emotional and meaningful connections.

Classroom as a Place

As educators in the early childhood classroom, we offer children a space to play, create, and learn. We follow regulations set forth by state licensing and

accrediting agencies about the areas or centers to be incorporated into the classroom (such as art, blocks, manipulatives, math, writing, and science). To establish and maintain high-quality early childhood programs, educators adhere to additional criteria outlined by observational tools such as the Early Childhood Environmental Rating Scale regarding the type, kind, and number of materials necessary to include in each area. Clearly, some materials, furniture, and equipment are necessary. Yet as design expert Jim Greenman notes in his book *Caring Spaces, Learning Spaces: Children's Environments That Work*, other factors are equally important to the space:

- What children do while in that space
- How they adapt the space to make it their own
- What social interactions and relationships are encouraged within the space

The moment when a space becomes a place is when children put their mark on it. For that moment in time, the child becomes empowered by the city she created in the block area or the dinner table he set in the home-living area. They personally enrich these areas by using the materials in their own ways and by having rich conversations and interactions with other children. When children shape, reconfigure, and align these spaces based on

84

their own cultural perceptions and life experiences, they gain deeply emotional connections with the environment.

Educators can help foster these relationships in many ways. You might add authentic objects such as models of fruits and vegetables indigenous to the neighborhood, name the shopping area after the local market, turn a wicker bowl into a chandelier hanging from the ceiling, or fill the kitchen buffet with real pots and pans purchased at a community resale shop.

The environment is invented by our presence in it, and we become one system, each influencing the other. Perhaps early childhood classrooms can be best thought of as sets of relationships organized and formulated by those who abide within the environment. If this is true, then children and adults do not experience classroom

environments—they create them. The environment is the space. What children create and the relationships they make within the space transform it into a place.

These transformations are not limited to the indoor classroom. The outdoor area is also changed, and the landscape is invented by our presence.

Read the story "Into the Forest" to see how young children reinterpreted the landscape of the nearby woods and made it their own.

Into the Forest: Creating a Place of Our Own

by Jacquelyn Weller, lead teacher, Child Development and Learning Laboratory at Central Michigan University

Being one who enjoys nature, I aspired to take a group of young children into the nearby forest for a year-round experience. Exploring the forest is about open, unplanned space. The forest space speaks differently from indoor spaces. It is engaging and inviting, gentle and peaceful, but also exciting and unexplored.

(continues)

After a short time in the forest, what used to be an unfamiliar space to the children began to be familiar and recognizable. Through repeated looking and exploring, they discovered the forest's wonders. The space became transformed by our visits—the landscape reinvented though the children's play. Intriguing conversations emerged while children discovered the stories already in the forest and also created new stories. As children settled into discovering the open and unplanned space of the forest, they began to create an assortment of different play stories.

"Hey, Elisha, it's time for dinner," Sofia said.

"We have to go cut trees down," Josh replied.

"Our boat broke because of the tornadoes," Dylan said.

"Do you want any ice cream?" Elisha asked.

"Who wants coffee? It's ready!" Sofia exclaimed.

"I am a mountain climber," Josh said.

Their play was creative, social, and imaginative. Through pretend play in the forest, the children were strengthening their problem-solving and language skills, as well as their social and emotional development. "I want it to be a house," Brandon said. "I want it to be a café," said Sofia. "Hey that's not the coffee shop, that's the fort!" Josh said as he walked inside the stick structure. The children debated back and forth until Sofia said, "Everybody stop! This can be whatever we want it to be. Brandon, if you want it to be a house, it can be a house. Josh, if you want it to be a fort, it can be a fort. And if we want it to be a café, it can be a café. It can be whatever you want it to be! We just have to take turns in here!"

As the children continued to make visits to the forest space, they strengthened their communication and imaginative skills. The children also

exhibited increased self-esteem and motivation to learn more about the forest.

Robin Moore, designer of environments for children's play, learning, and education, once said, "Natural spaces and materials stimulate children's limitless imaginations and serve as the medium of inventiveness and creativity." The open, unplanned space in the forest on the campus of Central Michigan University provided the children with this opportunity every time they stepped into this space.

The year came to an end, and the children's exploration and discovery of this open, unplanned space came to a close. What was once thought of as a space to visit became a destination place where relationships and friendships blossomed. It became a place they called their own. It will forever hold a place in their childhood memories.

Memories from the Back Porch

- - - - - - - - - - - - - - - - - -

by Paula Barnes, MS, owner of Resource Connections

When I was a child, I spent most summers at my grandparents' house. Being an only grandchild, I was often either in the kitchen helping to cook or bake, or outside playing in the backyard.

My grandparents—Pappaw and Nanny—raised chickens. The entire back part of the yard was occupied by chickens of all breeds and sizes. My Mammaw, who was my great-grandmother, lived with my grandparents until she passed away when I was about seven years old.

My favorite thing about going to stay at my grandparents' house was the back porch. I sat for many hours on that porch with my Mammaw while she braided my hair, told me stories of long ago, and dipped snuff. She even taught me how to spit! I remember sitting on top of the ice cream freezer while my Pappaw turned the crank and made the best homemade ice cream ever!

But the most fun happened under the porch. That's where the biggest earthworms were. That's where all of the mamma cats went to have their kittens. That's where the greenest, softest, and coolest moss grew too.

I played for hours and days on end under, around, and on that old porch with no more than the objects I found in the shed and the old dishes, utensils, pots and pans from my Nanny's kitchen. I made incredible mud pies! I cut that soft moss into sections to use as the carpet for my Barbie dolls. I searched for locust shells (Cicada exoskeletons) and collected as many as I could to use as make-believe pigs. I made pens for them out of sticks and used the sections of moss as their pasture.

I treasure those memories of playing under that porch—of wiggling and inching my way as far under and back as I could. It was a safe, cool, almost magical place where no one could fit but me!

Strategies for Transforming Spaces into Places

Be an Architect: Design Places for All Children

Think back to your childhood. Did you have a special space you could call your own? Maybe this space was outside in a tree house, under the front porch, or beneath an overgrown bush. Perhaps your special space was behind a curtain or inside a kitchen cabinet. Or maybe it was a quiet corner in the basement or attic.

Regardless of the location, you probably made the space your own by adding some of your most prized possessions and perhaps some comforts of home such as a blanket or pillow. Because you were in control of the space, you felt powerful and competent. You were the ruler of your kingdom. As teacher educators Ellen Lynn Hall and Jennifer Kofkin Rudkin note, childhood's special spaces are remembered decades later because these spaces give young children refuge from an adult-mandated world. For the most part, children live in spaces where they have little or no input. At home, the parent selects the child's bedroom furniture and determines where it is placed, decides the room color and the type of flooring, and chooses the wall décor. At school, the teacher selects the décor and arranges the furniture. In these adult-situated environments, children feel powerless and do not have a space to call their own. However, you can create emotion-centered spaces that children can call their own. Consider the following ideas as you get started.

Offer Empty Space

In most early childhood classrooms, every square inch is filled with equipment, furniture, or learning materials. There are no vacant spaces. Hall and Rudkin suggest offering at least one completely empty and undesignated space in your classroom. Do not give instructions to the children or share expectations for this empty space. Just provide it, and then watch how children use and interact with the space to reflect their own personal experiences and world views.

The Saul Spielberg Early Childhood Center (St. Louis, Missouri)

Create Habitats of Refuge

Early childhood classrooms are busy environments, and as Sandra Duncan and Michelle Salcedo note in a 2014 *Exchange* article, classrooms can sometimes feel as chaotic as Times Square in New York. Lights glare overhead. Noise is constant. Bright colors are everywhere. The smells can be overwhelming. Although adults can retreat from the hubbub—by

taking a quiet lunch break or going home—young children are more or less held captive in rooms that sometimes offer no escape and provide little refuge. But studies have shown that children value and sometimes prefer relaxed, calm, and comfortable places where they can simply be alone, according to researcher Kalevi Korpela. Although most early childhood classrooms offer at least one quiet space, this is often not enough. Multiple habitats of refuge are

needed where children have the space as well as the time to gain a sense of peace.

The cozy areas to the left were created by taking the door off the storage closet and placing a small rug, a few pillows, and box of books inside. Just the right size for one!

The characteristics of these habitats of refuge can vary depending on the child and the environment. You might set up a corner of the room with soft lighting and pillows, create a small, secluded area for one or two children, or drape some transparent fabric over a table or two chairs. No matter where the space is, the child is in control of the area, and adults are not welcome.

Understand the Child's Perspective

Architects and home designers carefully consider the inhabitant's perspective when creating blueprints and decorating the interior of a home. They think about the view from the front door, the positioning of the windows for the best view to the outside, and the placement of the home on the plot of land for morning and afternoon sun. These design experts plan for the best cabinet height or the dimensions of the kitchen island based on the space's size and shape. Every decision depends on the customer's needs and perspectives. Why shouldn't we, as designers of our classrooms, be equally attentive to children's perspectives?

The biggest factor influencing children's perspectives is their height. Young children live close to the ground in a world where everything seems gigantic. Surveying your classroom from their vantage point can help you understand what they see: Stand in the middle of your classroom and take note of what you see. Now kneel or sit in the same spot to get close to a child's height. You may notice distinct differences between what you were able to see from an adult height and from a child's height.

Adult Height View

Nature's Way Preschool (Kalamazoo, Michigan)

Child Height View

Rethinking the Classroom Landscape

Adults have more of a bird's-eye or all-inclusive view of the classroom than children, who have more of a restricted view and sometimes see only the sides of objects. Any furniture that is the height of the child and taller restricts the child from viewing the other parts of the room. Be aware of this limited view, and create environments where the view invites children to engage and interact. One strategy for creating better visual perspectives for children is to arrange smaller or shorter furniture in the middle of the classroom and place taller, larger equipment on the classroom's perimeter.

Elevate Children's Physical Comfort

Critically think about the physical surfaces in your classroom. For example, think about the children's options for sitting. Do you have seats other than the traditional chair designed to be used with a table? What is the ratio of hard seat surfaces to soft ones? Are the seats comfortable or institutional? Are there mostly seats designed for just one person or perhaps more? Does the room have a variety of seating arrangements with different heights, surfaces, and purposes? If not, try these ideas to add interest and comfort to the sitting spaces in your classroom.

- **Overstuffed chairs.** Find a Queen Anne's or overstuffed chair. Cut down the legs to make the chair a child's height (about 4 inches from the ground) and place the comfy chair in the reading or home-living center.
- **Claw-footed bathtub.** Fill an old-fashioned bathtub with pillows and a comforter. Add a basket of books, and it is a perfect spot to relax and enjoy a storybook with a friend.

Board of Jewish Early Childhood Centers at Beth Hillel B'nai Emunah (Winnetka, Illinois)

- **Hammock.** Hang a small hammock low to the ground; add pillows and an afghan for extra coziness and comfort.
- **Tree stumps.** Place a few tree stumps in a nook or out-of-the-way corner for small groups of children to gather and converse.
- **Couch.** Find a small couch with durable fabric or washable leather at a recycled-goods shop or garage sale. Add a few pillows or a small blanket. It's a great spot to share stories or read a book.

- **Rocker.** A rocker, whether child or adult sized, is a good seating option. Add a pad for warmth and comfort.
- **Stair risers.** Wide carpeted stairs provide children with several levels of seating. Little ones love to feel tall when they sit on the higher-level steps.
- **Ottoman.** An ottoman can provide comfy seating, especially if it is padded. Some ottomans have storage spaces, which is a bonus for the classroom.

message is uniformity, isolation, and separation from others. To promote collaboration and enhance social experiences for young children, consider how to create "we" spaces rather than the conventional "I" spaces. Intentionally including socially enhancing furniture and reconfiguring your physical space sends a powerful signal that participation and socialization are welcome, that connection with others is important, and that collaboration is powerful.

Include benches. Add benches to your classroom landscape—even at one of your activity tables. Benches promote conversations and socialization because they are designed for more than one person to sit and enjoy. They support open-ended possibilities for learning because they are not static, according to Bridgette Alomes, cofounder and CEO of play, Natural Pod. Benches "can be easily incorporated into play and learning by becoming a road, boat, construction platform, table, puppet theatre, or alpine ski hill," she notes.

Include several flexible gathering places. There is no perfect layout for the early childhood classroom. Some classroom design experts recommend

Be Intentional about Encouraging Socialization

According to Peter and Lucinda Barrett's research, humans receive powerful messages through their senses from their environment about how to act and behave. A person's behavior while at an outdoor rock concert, for example, would be completely different from that person's behavior when watching an opera in a world-famous concert hall. Likewise, children (consciously or not) internalize what the space tells them about how to act in the early childhood classroom. When children are assigned to a given chair, a particular spot or carpet square at story time, or made to sit in straight lines during group time, the inherent

planning environments in broad zones (such as dry, messy, active, and quiet) rather than focusing on smaller and detailed areas. Designers Scott Doorley and Scott Witthoft advise educators to think about the type of behavior the area would ideally support, for example, promoting small gatherings of children. Too often, early childhood classrooms have just one gathering area typically used for group or morning meeting time, and one is not usually enough, they advise. Young children need numerous areas to gather, collaborate, and converse. You can carve out and search for several miniature areas for children to gather by finding small nooks and crannies and then providing flexible and moveable pieces of equipment there. Procure some extra milk crates or foam cubes to use for informal small-group seating or as temporary dividers in the classroom. Try providing floor cushions or bean bags or purchasing furniture with casters for ease of movement. These options help create flexible and easily adapted environments. Also, if you attach casters to a large piece of furniture such as a sofa, you can easily reconfigure the space and transform the area into something totally unexpected or different.

Select round tables for social areas. The shape of furniture can affect socialization in the early childhood classroom. Square and rectangular tables—with their rigid corners and edges—have a more institutional feel. In contrast, circular tables tend to create

Image courtesy of Community Playthings

an increased sense of coziness. Socialization is more easily accomplished with round tables because children can make eye contact when they face each other, which inherently supports positive socialization. To increase opportunities for conversation in the home-living area, include a small round dining table designed to accommodate about four children.

Rethinking the Classroom Landscape

Gather around the campfire. Take a lesson from ancient storytellers. The campfire configuration promotes a sense of togetherness and can dramatically improve children's socialization and interaction. Erase the idea of sitting in straight lines on the carpet during group time. Get rid of the chairs. Instead, try sitting on the floor in a tight circle with you being and becoming an integral part of this circle. Unlike the traditional straight line configuration, children can see most of their classmates' faces rather than the backs or sides of their heads. Being able to see others at your own eye level promotes connectedness and awareness of group collaboration, according to Doorley and Witthoft.

More foot space, less shelf space. Children need room to social-ize—to tell their stories, pretend, and act out their real and fantasy lives. Give them room to move about, and provide more than one way to get in and out of an area. Children like to be able to see what is in an area before they move into it. They need more foot space and less shelf space.

Tight fit. Although the home-living center arrangement shown here looks cozy and inviting, it has little room for socialization. The area

appears to have various types of furniture needed for dramatic play in a kitchen: a stove, a refrigerator, a sink, a table and chairs, mops and brooms, a storage shelf, and a pantry. Yet it is ineffective because there is little room for children to successfully work, play, and socialize together within the confines of the center. When creating centers within your early childhood classroom, intentionally design the space to improve and enhance young children's socialization.

This home-living center has a lot of shelf space, but allows for minimal foot space. The area barely provides room for two children. Even with only two children

occupying the small space, they invariably will bump into each other because of the cramped conditions. Although there is a dining table for serving lunch or dinner, children rarely can sit down because it is challenging to pull out the chairs without knocking over or interfering with those playing at the sink or stove. When children do decide to eat at the table and sit down, there is no room for anyone else to move about the rest of the area. One design solution to this problem is to decrease the number of shelves or furniture in this area. That change would automatically increase the foot space and improve the chances for children to play together in small groups.

Inviting landscape. In the new arrangement, shown below, socialization is encouraged in the home-living center by providing more than one way to enter and exit, room to navigate around the area, authentic elements, and several different types of seating.

To increase the foot space in any of your learning centers, carefully consider every piece of equipment in the area and ask these questions:

- Why is this piece of furniture here? If you cannot immediately give a reason or purpose for the piece of furniture being in the area, it may be time to move it elsewhere (including out of the classroom).
  - Do I need this piece of equipment in this area? If you cannot immediately think of a specific need for the piece of equipment or if your answer was to define the space, eliminate it and clear more foot space.
  - Do children use this piece of equipment on a regular basis? Unless children use the item frequently, it is probably not needed in the space and could be removed.
  - Do I have at least one flexible piece of equipment in this area? Include flexible equipment that can do double duty (such as using an ottoman for both storage and sitting) to increase your foot space.

100

large tables, think about using tiny tables. Or exchange the large easel taking up floor space with a wall-hanging easel.

- Is this learning center the right size? Does the center's size correspond to the number of children typically using the area? Could the physical size of the center be larger to support increased foot space?
- Although the table in this home-living area is not round, it is small with equally tiny stools—perfect for a tea party with friends!

Design Multiple Ways to Enter and Exit an Area

In the photo of the home-living space with a tight fit (on page 99), children have only one way in and out of the learning center. That avenue is so small that it allows only one child at a time to enter or exit the area. Rather than using shelving units to define and surround the center, try having a rug define the space, as in the photo showing the more-inviting layout (on page 100). By doing so, you can create many ways children can come and go (especially with another friend) without hindrances or physically confining obstacles.

Infuse Authentic Elements

Authentic objects reflect children's real-life experiences. Because these objects are familiar, they spark young children's conversations and build interactions with others. Playing with authentic objects provides

- Could I find a smaller piece of equipment for the area? Unless an item is required by state agencies or licensing, consider alternatives. For example, you might replace the large, commercially purchased bookshelf with a basket to hold storybooks. Instead of

children a gateway to learning through their emotions. Children have increased ownership of objects in their classroom when they resemble known places in their lives. As they make connections to real life, children's language and conversations with others increase and friendships begin.

Children's Choice (Prince Albert, Saskatchewan, Canada)

Include Several Types of Seating Arrangements

In most home-living centers, the featured room is the kitchen and the only type of seating is at the dining table. Consider adding a living room to the home-living center. Include a couch, chair, occasional table, book basket, lamp, child-made television, and other items found in an authentic living room. By doing so, you add additional opportunities for socialization and small-group conversations.

Be an Illuminator: Create Islands of Light

Light is a powerful element in the early childhood environment. The presence of too much harsh light—especially florescent—can negatively affect children's health and behavior. Harsh light can lead to overstimulation, fatigue, and irritability, yet children who do not have enough light may end up squinting or losing concentration. Using light effectively in the classroom may foster appropriate behavior, concentration, learning, and even improved moods among children. Despite evidence showing the importance of light, a typical early childhood classroom has a fluorescent light fixture equipped with an on-off switch and no option for changing the intensity or level of light. Because few of us are electricians or have the financial support to make changes in the fluorescent lighting situation, consider some of the ideas that follow to ease your lighting challenges.

Place Lighting Strategically

Create multiple heights of illumination by adding different lamps that serve various levels of the classroom, such as the floor, the ceiling, and shelves. Consider some of the following options:

- Clamp lights
- Strip lighting
- Tea lights
- Hanging lamps
- Spotlights
- Glow lamps
- Overhead projectors
- Lava lamps
- Battery-powered lanterns
- Chandeliers
- Floor lamps
- Solar-powered lights
- Light tables
- Flashlights
- Table lamps
- Reading lights
- LED lights
- Octopus lamps
- Pole lamps
- Magnifying lamps

For example, an octopus-style lamp safely tucked behind a shelving unit creates general illumination for the manipulative or science areas. A clip-on lamp positioned over a writing table provides focused lighting needed for writing tasks.

Indirect illumination is a visual welcome—fostering an emotional sense of home—and it can provide a feeling of calm and stability, as illustrated in this image. The comfortable chair, small light, and natural elements combine to create a cozy atmosphere.

Enhance the classroom's mood with pools of light having different levels of lighting intensity. Determine the activity zones in your classroom and align light intensity accordingly. Whereas a block center demands full light, a cozy area requires a diffused and softer light arrangement.

Children's Home + Aid (Palatine, Illinois)

With the light table at an angle, the floor lamp tucked behind, and the plant safely protecting access to the lamp, the area shown here makes a perfect spot for a young child.

Another example is to use a table lamp with a three-way switch or dimmer to create a soft, calm mood for the library center. For safety reasons, affix the lamp to a shelf with heavy-duty, double-stick hook-and-loop tape or with hardware screws. Purchase lamps with protective lightbulb shields, and be sure cords are stored behind or under furniture and shelving units.

Capitalizing on Natural Light

If you are fortunate enough to have plenty of natural light from windows or skylights, consider keeping overhead fluorescent lights turned off and only using ambient lighting (such as from floor, pole, and table lamps). Also, do not let opaque objects block the sunlight from coming into the room.

In addition to being a source of natural light, treat windows as a sort of destination spot in your classroom—a place where children can go to see what's happening on the other side of the window. Because young children have a fascination with peering out windows, use this architectural feature as part of the daily activities such as math,

104

science, or writing. Windows provide an endless array of objects to observe, including people, birds, animals, vehicles, plants, and elements of weather. Examples of window activities include making a graph illustrating the number and color of birds seen in a week; sketching a favorite bird seen from the window; or writing a poem about the robin building a nest. In order to make the classroom window a destination spot, construct a window seat or offer wide carpeted steps so children have a birds-eye view of the outside world. Place comfortable seating or a table and chairs near the window.

One idea for transforming your classroom window into a destination spot is to add a window box directly outside the window and fill it with colorful flowers and herbs. Although you can purchase a window box at the local home improvement store, building a window box with children is a fun project. You can find instructions on the Internet for building a box (http://www.hgtvgardens.com/container-gardening/how-to-build-a-window-box). Before planting, determine the amount of sun that will cross your window box's path. (This is a great science project for children.) Plants that enjoy lots of sun (four to six hours) are poppies, verbenas, and zinnias. Forget-me-nots and coral bells are great choices for shady boxes (less than four hours of sun). Children are not the only ones who enjoy the classroom's window box; you will be pleased to see hummingbirds and butterflies stopping by for a drink from the flowers. So start making the windows the place where children want to go and want to be. Make your classroom windows a destination spot.

Promoting Sensory Engagement with Light

Providing experiences for young children to experiment with light is another strategy for adding illumination in the early childhood classroom. Manipulating light promotes kinesthetic and visual experiences. Children can experiment with lighting using some of the following equipment:

- Light tables
- Prisms
- Battery-powered candles
- Overhead projectors
- Disco balls
- Flashlights with colored cellophane over the lenses
- Light boxes
- Spotlights
- Slide projectors
- LED rope lights
- Nonbreakable mirrors

Children can enjoy many sensory experiences with gel beads and magnetic tiles.

For something different, you might try creating a small, but beautiful, light table by drilling a hole in a glass block and inserting electrical-approved LED lights, or you can use clear storage bins with lights.

One way to encourage curiosity and wonder is by letting children explore found nature items on a small light table.

You can get an interesting effect by letting children project images onto a thin piece of cloth with an overhead projector, creating an ever-evolving scene for all to enjoy.

and color—especially the color blue, which is a favorite of the female bowerbird.

Unlike the clutter manifested in many early childhood classrooms, the objects in these bowers are intentionally chosen for their value and purposefully placed. Far from institutional, each nest is a unique and artistic creation. Take a new look at your classroom through the eyes of a bowerbird and see how you can make your space more appealing, beautiful, and purposeful.

Be a Bowerbird: Display Children's Work with Honor

Native to New Guinea, the bowerbird may seem like an unlikely role model for teachers. However, as Sandra Duncan notes in a 2015 article in *Community Playthings*, this amazing avian artist and architect goes to extraordinary lengths to build and decorate his nest or bower.

Spending countless hours searching and collecting, the male bowerbird beautifies his habitat with broken bits of colorful glass, fragments of holiday garland and tinsel, shiny gum wrappers and milk caps, pieces of plastic and metal, tiny morsels of beautiful berries, and multicolored bits of yarn and string. His collections are painstakingly arranged according to type of material

Be a Curator

Dedicated to creating a welcoming and inviting space, the male bowerbird's reedy nest is more than a resting place; it is a beautiful habitat designed to attract the female bowerbird. The bird's natural impulse is to value his found objects by displaying them with great care. Each object brought to the nest area is highly cherished and positioned with intentionality.

The bowerbird arranges and displays his found treasures for aesthetic appeal, which is similar to the approach museum curators take when designing and arranging art exhibits. Curators determine how and where the priceless objects and artifacts will be displayed. They are the guardians of the artists' work. This is an invitation for you to become a guardian and curator of children's work. Celebrate and cherish their accomplishments as you would a fine piece of art.

Display children's work in attractive and beautiful ways. Be a bowerbird.

One way to honor children is to think critically about how you can display their work in ways that

respect their artistic accomplishments. Before you hang a child's work, a good rule of thumb is to ask this question: Would I hang this picture as it is in my home? If the answer is no, then it is important to ask yourself another question: What could I do to better honor this child's work?

Using a skirt or trouser hanger to display children's art projects works great!

Child Development and Learning Laboratory at Central Michigan University (Mount Pleasant, Michigan)

Rethinking the Classroom Landscape

One technique for showing the importance of a child's work is to make it gallery-presentable prior to hanging or displaying it. For example, try framing children's artwork with similar-type frames. Perhaps you could use unique textures such as burlap, grass cloth, or fabric for matting material. Or use different types of backdrops such as woven place mats or cork squares. Exhibit children's work in uncommon ways, such as using a chair with its legs cut down for a shelf, mounting a child's drawing on a large tree cookie, or inserting children's work and their photographs into an old windowpane that is backlit.

Another strategy for honoring children's work is to designate a specific area in the classroom designed to present their work in gallery-like fashion. Displaying children's work that is beautifully framed or exhibited recognizes and affirms its value to the artist, classroom community, and others who enter the space. Display with honor. Adopt this strategy as a fundamental approach to children's learning environments. Be a curator. Be a bowerbird.

Seek Beauty and Purpose

The male bowerbird makes intentional and informed choices when selecting objects to adorn his nest. Because he knows the female bird adores the color blue, he purposefully seeks out objects of that color. Shiny and glittery objects are also carefully selected to be an important and aesthetic part of his nest. Like the bowerbird, children need beauty in their spaces. Seek beauty, collect beauty, and create islands of beauty in your environment. Be a bowerbird.

Bowerbirds' nests are all unique. Just like early childhood classrooms, the birds' nests contain different objects, are individually arranged, and come in all shapes and sizes. Despite these differences, you can see the common denominator of beauty and purpose in each bird's nest. The male bowerbird intentionally selects beautiful objects for the nest with the purpose of attracting the female.

Make beauty and purpose your common denominator when making intentional choices to create spaces for young children. Some of these choices may be uncomfortable at first. As you focus on uniqueness and beauty, you will have to discard the assumption that all classrooms need to look alike. Your classroom

does not need to be a replica of the room next door or look like photos you see in early childhood catalogs. Being a bowerbird requires you to think beyond the ordinary.

Keeping in mind the goal of beauty and purpose, think critically about your classroom walls. Do you

Rethinking the Classroom Landscape

have more commercially purchased charts or more children's work displayed on the walls? Does an alphabet train or color chart remain posted the entire year? Are cartoon or storybook characters hanging up? Do you have brightly colored borders with scalloped edges around the bulletin board? Are most of the items on the walls laminated? If you answered "yes" to any of these questions, it is time for you to take some steps toward becoming a bowerbird.

Just like the bowerbird, be finicky about your classroom habitat—especially what is posted on your walls. One way to accomplish this is to decommercialize the space. Begin by taking everything off the classroom walls and bulletin boards. Now, like the bowerbird, mindfully and carefully select what items will or will not return to the wall. You can use the following guidelines:

- Most of the displays should be children's work. Limit commercially purchased materials (such as posters or charts) or cutesy cartoon figures.
- Create art galleries with clusters of pictures grouped together. To create interest and variety, arrange the grouping so each picture illustrates a different type of art medium (such as watercolors, chalk, or collage).
- Give children opportunities to create displays. Rather than purchasing an alphabet train, for example, have children make it. Children can create their own by using sticks, pebbles, clay, and small pinecones to construct the letters.

Besides reducing the commercial feel, consider reducing the clutter on your classroom walls. The male bowerbird has a distinct purpose for gathering objects to beautify his nest. With each carefully placed piece, he is sending a message to the female bird: You are important.

Look at what is hanging on your classroom walls. Have you carefully selected and placed each piece? Why are they important to be hanging in your classroom? What kinds of messages are they sending to the children?

Walls filled with commercially purchased charts and posters may send messages of indifference because they hang on the wall day after day and month after month. They may send messages of boredom if children are required to review their contents on a daily basis.

They may even send a message of "keep away" because children rarely are interactive with the laminated cardboard. In fact, laminated materials can create a harsh glare to children's eyes. Children with sensory integration disorders are challenged with this type of glare and often look away. Walls filled with commercially purchased charts and posters become nothing more than visual noise. And that noise is filled with unimportance.

Create walls of importance by taking down the laminated posters, number charts, the alphabet train, and even the commercially purchased calendar. Take down the neon-green paper backing and scalloped-edge borders from the bulletin board. Replace these with authentic and child-created objects that are purposefully and mindfully placed on the walls. Tell children that they are important. Be a bowerbird.

Look Critically at Your Classroom

According to research by Sandra Horne Martin, relationships can significantly improve when teachers intentionally design the physical environment in ways that promote positive interactions. Begin thinking critically about your classroom environment: Is it a space or a place?

There is an invisible yet powerful relationship between the physical structure of the classroom and

Board of Jewish Early Education Centers at B'nai Tikvah (Northbrook, Illinois)

the individuals who inhabit the environment. Use the following questionnaire to assess where you are and get your thought processes started about transforming your classroom landscape into an emotion-based place where relationships are nurtured, children's work is honored, and the environment is claimed by feelings.

Is Your Classroom Environment a Space or a Place?

Use this questionnaire to determine if your classroom provides children with a cookie-cutter institutional-type space or a place that is beautiful, respectful, and meaningful.

Directions: Select *A*, *B*, or *C* for each item listed below.
A = Strongly Agree
B = Agree
C = Strongly Disagree

_____ 1. An open and undesignated area provides opportunities for children to manipulate materials and equipment to transform the area into a place of their own.

_____ 2. In addition to the overhead lighting, illumination comes from at least two additional sources.

_____ 3. At least two objects of beauty (such as a honeycomb or fresh flowers) are exhibited to provoke a sense of wonder.

_____ 4. Children's displayed work outnumbers commercially purchased posters and charts.

_____ 5. The majority of children's work is displayed in attractive and beautiful ways using frames and unique textures such as burlap, grass cloth, or fabric for matting material.

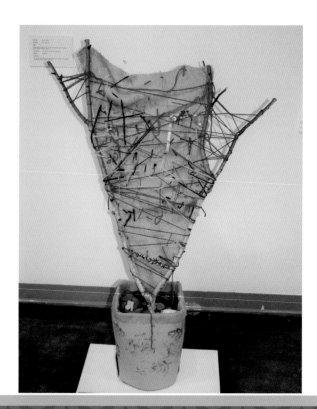

_____ 6. Children's work is exhibited in a gallery-type fashion.

_____ 7. At least two child-made works (such as an alphabet train or a calendar) created with authentic items (such as burlap, sticks, pebbles, clay, and small pinecones) are displayed in the classroom.

_____ 8. No more than five laminated or commercially purchased posters, pictures, or charts are posted in the classroom.

_____ 9. At least two designated areas in the classroom provide options for children who want to find a place of solitude or refuge.

_____ 10. The area provides at least three types of seating (such as cushions, an ottoman, or a couch), and at least two of the seats have soft surfaces.

Scoring:

This tool helps assess if your classroom is a space with an abundance of commercially purchased toys, materials, and furniture, or if it is a place that is beautiful, respectful, and meaningful to the children. Remember that the commitment to creating places for young children is an ongoing process of learning, so the goal is to improve over time.

If you responded frequently with an *A*, you are well on your way to creating a place that is a beautiful and respectful environment for young children.

If you responded frequently with a *B*, you may have some additional items needed to enrich your space in order for it to be considered a beautiful and respectful environment for young children.

If you responded frequently with a *C*, you may want to consider implementing some of the ideas in this chapter to transform your classroom space into a welcoming place.

4

Linking Geography to the Classroom: Topography, Flora, and Fauna

----

Forget not that the earth delights to feel your bare feet and the winds long to play with your hair.

—Khalil Gibran, *The Prophet*

Physical and Human Landscapes

From Niagara Falls to the Grand Canyon and the Everglades, the natural landscapes of the United States are of unparalleled and unmatched beauty. With more than 12,000 miles of coastline, our nation's landscapes are overflowing with majestic mountains, sweeping plains, soggy wetlands, cavernous canyons, and exquisite islands and peninsulas. We can view panoramic scenes of lakes, rivers, plateaus, woodlands, forests, deserts, salt flats, and waterfalls. America's physical landscapes are a beautiful tapestry of diverse topographies, climates, plants, and wildlife. Equally diverse, however, are the human landscapes of the United States.

Lake Michigan Sand Dunes

When is the last time you kicked off your shoes, took off your socks, and walked through freshly mowed summer grass or dug your toes into a sandy beach? When is the last time you took a nap on the ground with crunchy autumn leaves tickling your legs and arms, sunk your feet in a muddy lake bottom, or stomped barefoot through a mud puddle? Can't remember when?

Much like America's physical landscapes, its human landscapes are equally beautiful and diverse. The United States has more than 300 million inhabitants, with more than 150,000 different last names and 5,000 different first names, according to the Census Bureau. Nationalities from all over the world are represented. Each person's physical characteristics, experiences and backgrounds, cultures and heritages, and personalities and spirits are as unique as their thumbprints. However, amid the diversity of physical and human landscapes, there is one common denominator—the ground beneath our feet.

Engaging in these simple pleasures could give your health and well-being a big boost, so it might be time to take off your socks and shoes. Being in direct physical contact with Mother Earth may help you feel calmer, lower your stress hormones, improve your heart rhythms, lessen your muscle stiffness, reduce inflammation, lower blood pressure, improve your mood and self-esteem, increase your immune responses, and even help you sleep better. Human beings simply seem wired to live better physically, mentally, and emotionally with a steady influx of nature. And the benefits of connecting or grounding with the earth are not just limited to adults but also extend to children.

Connecting with Mother Earth

Grounding or *earthing* is defined as placing the human body in direct contact with the land whether it happens to be grass, dirt, mud, water, sand, or other natural elements. Connecting to the earth is not a new concept—virtually all of our ancestors did it. For most of our history, humans experienced an intimate connection with the earth. We slept on the ground with animal skins for warmth. Our abodes had dirt floors, and we walked the land with bare feet. It is only recently that plastics, asphalt, steel, and wood have separated us from direct contact with the land.

Today's children tend to be ungrounded. As Mary Rivkin notes in her book *The Great Outdoors*, "Children's access to outdoor play has evaporated like water in sunshine." The Environmental Protection Agency estimated in 2014 that American adults tend to spend as much as 93 percent of their lives indoors.

Photo courtesy of Jacquelyn Weller

Children spend significantly less time outside than previous generations. The long hours of outdoor explorations are a quickly vanishing aspect of contemporary childhood. Yet multiple research studies indicate that children who spend time interacting with nature are healthier, happier, and do better in school. So it is important for early childhood educators to provide plenty of experiences for children to play in the great and wild outdoors.

Earthing or grounding gives children a chance to physically engage with the world around them. For most, it's simple to give children grounding opportunities

Rethinking the Classroom Landscape

because nature is all around us; just step outside and engage the senses and the mind. This doesn't mean children need to play in the mud every day. It might be as simple as sitting in the grass and placing your feet on its cool blades or spilling beach sand over your feet to cover them up only to find a few toes peeking out. It might be as easy as holding a smooth river rock plucked from a spring stream in your hands and feeling the absorption of the heat from your body. Whatever natural element you explore, make sure to touch, see, smell, and listen. After all, isn't that the way we all learn best—through our senses?

> " Unexpected pleasures are still the best. The pliant, inviting texture of moist grass, the ripping sensation when roots separate from the earth, the mingled smell of soil, dirt, and vegetation—all of these make an imprint on the child's heart.
> —**Molly Dannenmaier**, *A Child's Garden*

Earthing does not cost a penny. It's not complicated, and the rewards of bonding with the earth are enormous for adults and young children.

Nature's Way Preschool (Kalamazoo, Michigan)

Earthing Experiences

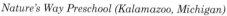

- Stomp in a puddle
- Climb a tree
- Walk barefoot in the early morning dew
- Bury your toes in mud
- Run barefoot through a water sprinkler
- Watch clouds while lying on your back in the grass
- Play in the dirt
- Look for creatures under a rock or in the grass
- Splash in the rain

- Wade through a shallow stream
- Feel a tree's bark, branches, and leaves
- Gather interesting sticks from the ground
- Look for a four-leaf clover
- Build sand castles on the beach
- Collect pinecones
- Float a leaf on a puddle of water
- Hold a dandelion and blow upon it
- Toss autumn leaves in the air

Getting Grounded

Many people believe that spending time in nature is just as important for optimal health as good nutrition, exercise, and a moderate lifestyles. Perhaps good health may be as easy as a walk in the park! Unfortunately, today's children are growing up in a concrete and asphalt world. Because children spend most of their time sitting indoors in classrooms, staying inside at home, or riding in cars and school buses, many young children are isolated from the earth. Even if they do go outside, children typically wear boots, shoes, sandals, or flip-flops, creating a plastic or man-made barrier between the bottoms of their feet and the earth. It is important, therefore, to give children opportunities to physically connect with the outside environment and the ground they walk on. As educator Rae Pica notes in her book *What if Everybody Understood Child Development?* "When we limit outdoor play, we ignore what we know about who children are and how they learn and grow. Why do we believe we can do better than what nature intended or that we can improve on nature's design? Are we so obsessed with what we perceive as 'achievement' that we're willing to have our children give up everything else, including joy, imagination, connection with nature, and even physical fitness, to attain it?"

Anything attached and rooted to the earth—such as trees, plants, bushes, flowers, vines, and even grass—is grounded. So go outside and begin earthing by trying some of the ideas suggested here.

Building Nests!

There had been lots of discussion and conversation about the topic of birds in the Chippewa Nature Center preschool classroom. As the children gathered outside at stump circle, there was talk about what to do on today's hike. They decided to be mommy and daddy birds and needed to build nests for their baby birds. Along with the teachers, children flapped their way into the woods. Once the children found a spot with lots of natural loose parts, they stopped and promptly found a good place to construct the baby bird nests. Along the way, children and teachers talked about camouflage, protecting their eggs, prey, and predators. The children were ingenious in figuring out how to protect their eggs from predators—even flying and placing the egg far away from the nest. This activity grounded children as they experienced the sight, sound, smell, and touch of the earth.

What shall we do on today's hike?
Let's flap our way into the forest!
This is the perfect place for the nests.

We have to hide the baby eggs from the many predators of the forest.

Oh no! It's a predator! But don't worry, mama and daddy birds hid their eggs in a safe spot.

What great fun and learning! Now it's time to fly back home.

Space Traveler

- - - - - - - - -

by Steve Erwin, early childhood specialist

How do children decide what to observe in nature, what captures their attention, makes them stop, ask questions, and wonder? In forty years of working with children, I do not think I fully comprehended or completely engaged my thoughts to these questions until I took a walk with a two-year-old, who I will refer to as my space traveler.

While working at a university child development lab, I met an inquisitive two-year-old boy. Each week, the children would take a nature walk around the beautiful campus located in the city's park system. Walking with an assigned teacher, I noticed my space traveler was always lagging behind the rest of the children. My curiosity was piqued, and I wondered what was capturing his attention and time, so I volunteered to walk with him.

As we set off on our walk, he immediately was intrigued with a large root pushing up through the sidewalk . . . a chattering squirrel . . . a nubby stick . . . buzzing bees in a bottle brush tree . . . and a tiny pinecone. Being only two, he did not have all the words to communicate his observations, but his facial expressions, interested eyes, and slow intentional walking pace told the whole story as the stage was set for many discoveries along the path. When the space traveler and I finally arrived at the creek, I noticed that the rest of the children were way ahead of us because nothing could get by him. He even noticed a line of small ants traveling alongside the path and patiently watched them march until they reached a large broken oak limb perched next to the creek.

I cannot remember all of the observations made, but I do remember the space traveler's fierce interest, pure delight, and total satisfaction of his travels through space. Yes, we were last by 20 minutes, but what is time when you can enjoy the toddler's view and reaction to the natural world—a view of a traveler in space?

Going Barefoot

It helps to remove man-made barriers separating children from physically connecting to the earth. On warm summer days, let children take off their shoes and socks and have story time outside under a tree. During a spring shower, you can walk barefoot through the rain. If you live in the city or in an area where there is not a piece of grass or land, don't worry! Cement is a semiconductor of the earth's energy, so go ahead and walk barefoot, create sidewalk chalk art, or play barefoot hopscotch on the sidewalk.

Mucking in Mud

Children engage deeply in play with all natural elements, but especially with mud. It is one of the most readily accessible natural elements available to children all over the world, and lends itself to multitudes of learning opportunities in one form or another. Creativity is at its best when children are given mud—a material that has no specific use, is completely open ended, and lends itself to the contours of children's hands with ease and grace. Mud is a living substance interacting

> In Just—
> spring when the world is mud-
> luscious . . . and it's
> spring
> when the world is puddle-wonderful.
> —**e.e. cummings,** "In Just—"

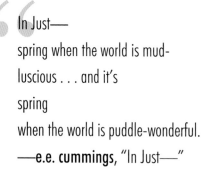

Special Blessings Child Care (Emporia, Kansas)

might go to your childhood and all the joyous connections you made with magical mud. Then again, your thoughts may go to the effort and time it takes to clean up children who are covered in mud from head to toe. Even though mud play is increasingly recognized as a significant part of a child's learning day, we also hear of parents describing their offspring as inside children. Becoming dirty—much less muddy—may not be something that ever happens for them. Teachers also often approach the idea of playing in a mud hole or creating a mud kitchen with much trepidation and with some level of confusion as to the reasoning for such an addition to the outdoor space.

with another living substance. Mud is life connecting with life. Mud puddles are places where magic can happen. Mud soothes and comforts because it is unassuming and is willing to do, be, and respond to whatever the child desires.

The inclusion of mud play and mud kitchens in the daily outdoor experiences of young children is a newly defined way of offering kinesthetic experiences with an element of the earth. The idea of mud play, however, conjures up conflicting images, positive and negative. When considering the pros and cons of mud play, your thoughts

Today's researchers and early learning experts are examining the benefits and connections children are making while playing freely with the magical combination of earth and water. Could it be the divine consistency itself that wakes up a long-forgotten memory within us? Could it be that we have an innate understanding of the properties of the earth itself?

Does the inherent scientist within the child's ever-curious mind seek the sights, scents, textures, flavors, and sounds of the earth itself?

Children playing in mud engage deeply with the substances of earth and water as they imagine themselves to be scientists, chefs, construction workers, engineers, and any assorted members of a family or community. With each new role, children practice new skills, learn more about nature, and gain knowledge about the essence of mud. Perhaps these elements of water and dirt come together to support children's learning of the world in a deeply profound manner. Perhaps something as simple as mud can ground

Chippewa Nature Center's Nature Preschool (Midland, Michigan)

Special Blessings Child Care (Emporia, Kansas)

Mud Pies and Messes

by Nancy Alexander, director of Northwestern State University Child and Family Network

A Preschool Experience

Helping a friend, Judy, conduct her version of field day for her preschool, I was assigned to supervise the mud area. This was a low area of the playground, which she had dug out even more, filled with water from a nearby hose, and in the interest of limited cleanup facilities, had placed a board across the self-made ditch to protect shoes.

Parents were an integral part of this day, and two mothers were assigned to the area with me. It was soon very clear why Judy had asked me to take on this particular role. We gathered at our assigned spot about ten minutes before the children came out. The two mothers were clearly concerned about how this was going to work and openly expressed their chagrin about muddy children and messiness. Feeling their negative vibes, I tried to communicate how much fun the children would have but they were not convinced. As two four-year-old boys came to the area, the careful orientation Judy had provided was apparent. The boys were careful to

stay on the board bridge while enjoying the texture and properties of the mud. As we staffed our post, the conversation of the two mothers turned to their own experience making mud pies as children. In a very short time, their observations of the children's joy won them over.

A School-Age Experience

In an afterschool program, mud play was a popular activity. We set up the activity on a small table with an assortment of pans, muffin tins, and assorted mud-pie-making paraphernalia. We had no convenient water source and relied on filled gallon milk jugs for our water supply. An area of the

playground where grass did not grow provided what the children referred to as "clean dirt," meaning it was free of leaves and sticks.

The water routine was that when a jug was empty it was put near the back steps to be filled again for the next day. In order to make sure that water got to where it was needed, the three jugs used in rotation were marked clearly with a Sharpie, "Mud Pie Water." That differentiated them from the art water and the bubble solutions to ensure that water was always available where required. Visiting parents often asked how mud pie water was different from plain water or even art water, amused by our explanation.

A scavenged wooden pallet was placed for children to stand on to avoid standing in the muddy puddle that inevitably developed. While this area was extremely popular on most days, we did notice an interesting phenomenon. After a few days of use, children didn't go into the mud area. Our first efforts centered on encouraging children to go there but usually with few takers. Finally, one little girl solved the puzzle. Using that matter-of-fact tone that says "you adults really ought to know this," she said, "Well, it's just TOO messy," putting great emphasis on the *too*. Realizing that even mud play is more appealing when attractively displayed, we set aside Fridays as cleanup day. We brought in hoses for the children to wash down the area, so it was clean and fresh for the upcoming week. We restocked the clean dirt (freshly dug), made sure plenty of fresh water was handy, and stocked clean accessories. We made sure the mud pie water was clean and fresh. Once again, the mud pie area became a vital part of the outdoor experiences.

Special Blessings Child Care (Emporia, Kansas)

Mud Pies and Beans

----

by Sue Penix, preschool nature outreach specialist

When I was a young child, the neighborhood children would gather to play on a vacant lot in back of our townhouses. This lot had a little grass and some wildflowers, a few trees, and several dirt patches with different colored dirt. There was black dirt, greenish-grey dirt, and brown dirt. A small patch of sand and pale yellow dirt mixed together was under one of the trees. On one end of the field, the remains of an old foundation from a garage captured our imaginations. The garage foundation became our castle, fortress, school, and—on most days—our play house.

Each of us would bring different loose parts from home with which to play. Some would bring dolls and strollers, others brought pots and pans, spoons, empty containers, and water. We would then use the different colored dirt, grass, dandelions, clover flowers, and sticks and stones to create mud-pie meals for our dolls and each other. We would make up recipes for different dishes such as baked beans, which was a mixture of brown dirt, small pebbles (beans), and various spices to flavor the beans. Spices were a combination of grass, flowers, and a little yellow dirt. The concoction was mixed up, poured into a pot, and cooked on our imaginary stove. We spent countless hours of uninterrupted play on the vacant lot and gained a lifetime of memories. As adults, some of us turned out to be pretty good at making baked beans.

the expense required—not to mention the demand for maintenance and upkeep such as watering, weeding, and mulching. If the idea of a large garden isn't for you, creating a miniature garden may be appealing. These gardens fit in small spaces inside or outside, and they are inexpensive and easy to create.

A minigarden could also be thought of as a garden in a container. It doesn't matter if your classroom is in the city, suburbs, country, or somewhere in between; you can grow a garden. In the book *Roots, Shoots, Buckets, and Boots: Gardening Together with Children*, Sharon Lovejoy notes, "You don't need land, or very much space, but you do need a sense of humor,

children to the earth. You may find that creating a special space such as a mud hill, hole, or kitchen is well worth the time and effort.

Growing Miniature Gardens

Growing a garden is a great way to connect with the earth. The process of digging, planting, watering, and harvesting gives children opportunities to experience the varied textures, smells, and sights of nature. Oftentimes, however, early childhood teachers shy away from large gardens because of limited space and

a good imagination, light, soil, water, a collection of containers and plants. Once you're hooked on gardening in containers, you will look at things differently. Common castoffs and whimsical objects tantalize you into designing a medley of unusual, easy-to-care-for gardens." You might try using some of the following items for container gardens:

- A colander
- Rain boots
- A watering can
- An RV sink
- Garden gloves
- A barrel
- A garden hat
- A metal teapot
- A flat-bottomed purse
- A wheelbarrow
- A wagon
- A ceramic bowl

Happy Faces II Academy (Fredereiksted, Virgin Islands)

Boot Gardens

What about a boot garden? Most families have an old pair of shoes or boots they are ready to pitch in the garbage or send to recycling. Instead of throwing them away, ask families to contribute their old shoes— especially rain boots—to the classroom. Children can decorate boots, fill them with dirt, and plant flowers, herbs, vegetables, or fruits. If you place the filled boots by the front entryway, you can create a cheerful and welcoming display.

CD Gardens

An empty CD case makes a great minigarden for young children because the plant's growth process is

Peifer Elementary School (Schererville, Indiana)

Rethinking the Classroom Landscape

Downtown Baltimore Child Development Center
(Baltimore, Maryland)

so visible. It is usually not too difficult to collect enough cases from families, friends, neighbors, and relatives for every child to have their own garden.

Toy Truck Gardens

Using toy trucks or cars as containers, you can create an interesting and unique space to plant flowers. Scout out toys at the local resale shop or garage sales. Think outside of the box when looking for containers for minigardens.

Tin Can Gardens

Collecting tin cans from the local community, families, and even your own kitchen is easy. Simply prepare the tin cans for the children's plantings by washing and disposing of any cans with sharp edges. Because cans with lids do not have sharp edges, they work best for planting projects.

Hint: With a hammer and nail, punch a hole in the top of the can. After children have planted their flowers or vegetables, thread a piece of wire or chain through the hole, and hang it on a nail on a fence or nearby tree.

holes. If you help younger children get started, they can cut the holes with children's scissors.

4. Fill with potting soil and plant various types of flowers, herbs, or other plants in the bottle.

5. Using fishing line, string, or thin wire, you can hang the water bottle gardens from a branch or in the window to make a beautiful nature display.

Cardboard-Tube Garden

Take a paper towel cardboard tube and cut it into four even sections. One cardboard tube will make four minigardens. At the end of each of the sections, cut four

Water Bottle Gardens

Plastic water bottles seem to be everywhere you look. Why not make good use of them by having children transform these landfill hazards into beautiful minigardens?

It's easy for children to make these bottle gardens with a few simple steps:

1. Gather empty water bottles.
2. Take the labels off the bottles and wash them. This is a great project for the water table.
3. Cut two holes on opposite sides of the bottles; make them large enough so that the plants can grow out of the

Taltree Arboretum (Valparaiso, Indiana)

138

slits about 1 inch high. Then, fold the flaps and overlap them as you would when putting together the bottom of a cardboard box. Tape that end only. Fill with dirt and place a small plant in the cardboard tube. Once the minigardens have been displayed in the classroom for a while, children can plant them in the ground or in a classroom garden. Because the cardboard tube is biodegradable, it is a perfect planter!

Plant and Flower Selection

When deciding what plants to put in children's gardens, think quick-growing. Children like to see almost immediate results from their gardening efforts. They also enjoy seeing interesting features in plants, such as flowers that look like faces, and exploring fragrances, textures, and colors.

Taking an excursion with the children to the local nursery, searching through seed packets, or browsing a flower catalog so they can help select the appropriate flowers for their garden can help elevate their commitment and interest in the garden.

Some plants that are popular with children include pumpkins, beans, pansies, strawberries, radishes, sunflowers, tomatoes, gourds, and snapdragons. See

Easy-to-Grow Plants and Flowers

Perennials (Plants live for several years)	**Annuals** (Plants live for only one growing season)
Daylily Requiring full sunlight, these colorful flowers are easy to grow. They spread in a flower bed and can be transplanted to fill in new areas.	Zinnia These bright and colorful plants are easy to grow. Zinnias attract some types of butterflies, such as skippers, to the garden also.
Nasturtium This plant is a vibrant addition to the children's garden and its flowers and leaves are edible. Nasturtiums grow in full sun, and you can hang them in baskets or let children grow them at ground level.	Sunflower This bright-yellow plant has a big daisy-like flower face and a brown center that ripens with seeds, which can be baked as a snack. Sunflowers tolerate heat and water well.
Marigold This plant grows quickly, so children do not have to wait long to see the results of their work. Marigolds enjoy sun.	Pansy With its cheery face, this plant is a favorite with young children. Colorful pansies can be used as a garnish on pancakes.

Note: Use caution as some of these plants can cause allergies, skin irritation, or upset stomach in some people.

the table on the next page for several easy-to-grow perennials and annuals.

Caution: Whatever plants and flowers you choose to grow, be sure they are nontoxic and not poisonous.

Jack Be Little pumpkins are also easy-to-grow plants. Young children are charmed by their miniature size as they only grow to be 3 or 4 inches

in diameter. Jack Be Little pumpkins are terrific for decorating or eating. Don't be fooled by their name, however. The Jack Be Little is actually a gourd and not a pumpkin!

Worm Garden

Making a worm garden is a fun and easy gardening activity for young children. You can follow these easy steps, asking the children to help:

1. Find a clear plastic jug or container. A quart-sized glass jar will also work.
2. If your playground or backyard has dark soil, you can dig some up. Or you can purchase potting soil to use.
3. Gather worm bedding, which consists of compost, rotting tree leaves, flowers, or plants.

4. Fill the container about halfway by alternating several loose layers of soil and worm bedding. You can also alternate layers of sand and soil, ending with a top layer of worm bedding.
5. You will need three or four compost worms, which you can buy online or dig up in your own patch of land. Sometimes after a rain on a warm spring day, you can find earthworms crawling about in the grass or sidewalks. Add the worms to the top layer in the container.
6. Spray the leaves or compost with water.
7. Secure the container with either its lid or plastic wrap. Punch a few holes in the lid or wrap for air circulation.
8. Wrap the container with black paper and place in a cool spot. After a few days, take off the paper to see the tunnel and burrowing work of the worms.

A larger worm garden can also be made out of other containers such as a fish aquarium or a long plastic storage box about 3 feet long by 2 feet wide by 1½ feet high. Using a clear container allows children to see the tunnels and the work of the earthworms. Punch holes in the sides of the container for aeration. Because the worm garden should be kept moist at all times, make a drainage area in the bottom of the bin. Use large rocks or a rigid divider to keep the drainage area separate from the worms' living and working space. Loosely cover the worm garden to keep the moisture in. Since worms are nocturnal, keep the container in a darker area of the classroom. Worms prefer cool environments, so keep them out of the sun.

Feed the worms well-chopped vegetable matter mixed with a bit of water. Worms also enjoy small amounts of fruit scraps such as peels, rinds, and cores. They prefer softer foods. Do not feed meat, bones, oils, or dairy products to the worms. Limit the amount of soft food scraps given to the worms. Do not overfeed. If the food is not consumed by the worms in twenty-four hours, reduce the amount of scraps you are putting in the bin.

To maintain the worm garden, you will need to feed and water the soil, and mix it up on a regular basis. In order for the worms to get enough air, the soil needs to be fluffed up about once a week. If the dirt begins to get dry, spray with a water bottle. If the soil gets too wet, try adding strips of newspaper to the dirt.

For more information on how to construct a worm bin and grow worms, you can visit Nature Explore's website (www.natureexplore.org/wormbin).

Tall-Grass Garden

Have you ever stood in a field of tall grass—especially with the wind blowing softly? The experience is mesmerizing and magical for adults and young children. Tall grass is a place of childhood: to explore, to play, and to be. Crouching in the grass and hiding from your friends never gets old because of the excitement of hunting, being hunted, and finding clever spaces.

When we think of tall grasses, we often think of large sprawling fields. Because young children are explorers and find joy in the smallest of things, you don't have to have a field of tall grass. A small spot will do. Here are a few tips for selecting and growing ornamental grasses suitable for young children:

- Select grasses that are soft and feathery.
- Plant grasses of different heights.
- Be sure the height of the grasses will not be too high. Children should feel safe in exploring, and you should be able to see the children from your height.
- For a meadow-like effect, scatter prairie grass seed. Once the grass has grown high enough, mow a path through it. Even though the path may not feel long to you, it will to a young child.

Make sure you choose grasses that are safe for the children in your care.

Herb Garden

Growing herbs in a minigarden can be an exciting activity for young children. Local garden shops, green grocers, greenhouses, and farmer's markets can give you ideas, suggestions, and hints on how to grow herbs. To start a child-friendly herb garden, you might begin with a pizza garden. Make your garden plot into the shape of a circle—just like a pizza! Divide each planting

Miniature Garden Growing Tips

- Choose a garden site that gets at least six hours of sun a day.
- If the land has never been a garden before, dig and turn the ground over for about 8 inches deep.
- If space is at a premium, design parts of your garden vertically by using a trellis to support plants growing upward (such as pole beans, cucumbers, and squash).
- Because water is an important component of successful gardening, be sure to locate your garden near a source of water.

area into a wedge and plant herbs appropriate for a pizza (for instance, thyme, cilantro, or parsley). Also include plants such as tomatoes, bell peppers, and onions. Herbs are easy to grow, fun to harvest, and good to eat. Of course, you will need to choose herbs that are safe for young children, and you should be aware that some popular herbs are not.

Garden with Wings (Butterfly Garden)

Children are fascinated by butterflies, especially their graceful movements, beautiful colors, and fluttering wings. One way for children to experience and enjoy seeing these lovely creatures is to build a butterfly garden outside the classroom door or window. It's simple to do: just offer a place for caterpillars and adult butterflies to munch and rest. Attract caterpillars and butterflies by growing plants that they like to eat (host plants) and feed on (nectar plants).

Plants that are good for butterfly gardens include the following:

- Butterfly milkweed
- Aster
- Nasturtium
- Sunflower
- Dill
- Fennel
- Parsley
- Pineapple sage
- Blue shasta daisy
- Chives
- Butterfly bush
- Parsley

Butterfly gardens can be any size—from a small window box to a grand area encompassing many square feet of land. Regardless of the size, consider the elements you need to include to attract butterflies and caterpillars to your space.

Trees and shrubs not only provide shade but also protect the garden from the wind; they make it easier for butterflies to explore the garden. Trees and shrubs make a good roosting and hiding place for butterflies and also provide tasty snacks for caterpillars.

Butterflies need a source of water. Although they enjoy rainwater and dew, they also need water from mud puddles. Because puddles absorb salt and nutrients from the earth, they are important to the health of butterflies and are necessary components in butterfly gardens. That is why you often see butterflies flying and swarming around mud puddles. This process is called puddling.

Sunlight is important because butterflies cannot fly when they are extremely cold. They are cold-blooded creatures that need to warm their bodies in the morning sun, so it is best to locate the butterfly garden where sunlight will reach ground level early in the day. One idea is to position large rocks where they are easily exposed to the morning sun so the rocks quickly absorb its warmth. Or position the garden near a sidewalk or pavement that gets at least six hours of sunlight each day.

Another important aspect of creating a butterfly garden is to determine the species of butterflies

indigenous to your area so you can include appropriate plants, shrubs, and trees. To find out, visit a nursery, nature center, or botanical garden in your community, and talk with experts. You can also conduct online research (try http://www.thebutterflysite.com/) to determine the best plant life for a butterfly garden in your neighborhood.

Let children help design and create the classroom's butterfly garden. After researching butterflies indigenous to your area, you can look on the Internet for images of these butterflies that you can print out. Then find images of the plants, flowers, trees, and shrubs that attract these species and print those out. Involve children in the process of designing the garden. Get a large piece of butcher paper, and outline an area to represent the garden's blueprint. Let children experiment with placing the pictures of the plants and flowers on the blueprint to see how they could fit in the space. Keep the blueprint in your science area for a few days so everyone has an opportunity to participate in the design of the butterfly garden. Invite parents to help too. If you get adults and children involved at the start, you are likely to have more physical help when actual construction begins.

Extend the design process by discussing specific plants and flowers and identifying what they need to grow and how tall they will grow. Determine which plants will work best in particular areas of the garden.

Visiting a nearby greenhouse to select and purchase the plants and flowers can add to the butterfly garden experience. Constructing butterfly houses, adding nectar sources, and building fairy houses for will make the experience magical.

Creating Nature Art

Children are natural gatherers, foragers, and guardians of small precious finds. So take them outdoors, walk down a pathway and into natural places, and watch as their senses and curiosity awaken. Encourage children's curiosity by providing many opportunities to collect and find beautiful objects from the natural world. Before you set off to explore wild spaces, give each child a small basket or paper bag in which to gather their found objects (such as twigs, rocks, mosses, pinecones, buckeyes, and dandelions). Not only will children want to keep their treasures, they will most likely come back again and again revisiting and examining the bag's contents. For bigger finds, bring a wagon or strap to tie up larger branches or twig bundles. Also bring along a reporter's bag filled with documentation, observation, and other useful tools for children to record their explorations and document their findings.

You can make a reporter's bag using a canvas tote bag or something similar, and stocking it with items such as a butterfly net, a container for catching

place items on the acrylic sheet so they can view the underside, use binoculars to view elements of nature that are farther away, document their findings on paper, and more! For safety, caution children never to look directly at the sun.

Also, let children know that they should not pick up small live insects and bugs. However, you can encourage them to observe these small creature's habitats without disturbing them. Explain to the children that we can all care for and protect the creatures living in these wild places. It is important for children to understand that natural environments are shared environments, and we all must learn to care for the creatures whose homes we are visiting.

and releasing small critters, a magnifying glass, a sketch pad and writing tools, a camera, a small sheet of acrylic glass, binoculars, and a strainer. For safety, caution children not to look directly at the sun using any of these viewing tools. Children can capture insects using the butterfly net, examine small animals in the catch-and-release container with the magnifying glass, scoop up items from a creek in the strainer,

Bringing the found treasures back into the classroom is as much of an adventure as actually finding them. Encourage children to examine the objects they found and perhaps sort by characteristics. Because children are fascinated by small details, they may classify their treasures in surprising ways. It might be all of the found objects with round black spots . . . those with gnarly nubs, or ones with spidery-looking bumps.

Image courtesy of Community Playthings

Rethinking the Classroom Landscape

> The ground we walk on, the plants and creatures, the clouds above constantly dissolving into new formations—each a gift of nature possessing its own radiant energy, bound together by cosmic harmony.
> —Ruth Bernhard

Once children have gathered, explored, and classified their individual found objects, they can display their treasures on a large surface (such as the sidewalk, the floor, or a table) for others to see and enjoy.

An opportunity for group display provides a special time for many rich discussions on children's choices. But collecting and displaying children's found objects is not enough. After sharing stories, encourage children to think about ways to keep or preserve their precious nature finds for at least a week or so. Offer suggestions such as collaborative projects as well as individual projects. Some examples of nature construction projects

Hope's Home (Prince Albert, Saskatchewan, Canada)

Milgard Child Development Center (Puyallup, Washington)

are mobiles, sculptures, canvas art, stepping-stones, collages, and murals. By working with natural items, children learn about the different textures, smells, and colors in a way they will remember. By giving children many opportunities to make nature art, you will help them feel like experts about items such as tree bark, river stones, pine needles, seed pods, and leaves.

Hand-Printed Nature

Nature is a showcase of patterns, colors, and textures. As artist and gardener Laura Bethmann notes in her book *Hand Printing from Nature*, children can capture "direct impressions of life" using a simple technique. "Freshly picked bits of nature—carefully inked and pressed to paper, fabric, and other surfaces—make

Ganero Child Development Center at Pierce College (Puyallup, Washington)

150

Children's Choice (Prince Albert, Saskatchewan, Canada)

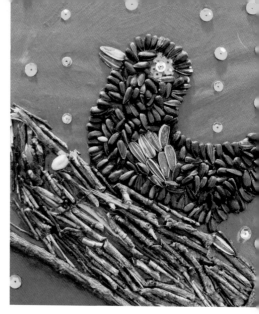

The Adventure Club (Dyer, Indiana)

Flowers have patterns of color.

life-size mirror images of them. The forms, patterns, and textures of flowers, leaves, roots, wood grain, fruits, vegetables, feathers, shells, and a host of other found objects can produce phenomenally detailed expressive art," she asserts. Out of sensitivity to children who may have food-insecurity challenges, however, you may want to avoid printing with edible objects. You should also be sensitive to children's allergies when choosing natural objects as art materials.

Wood has a pattern of round lines.

Linking Geography to the Classroom: Topography, Flora, and Fauna

Getting started with hand printing is easy because objects from nature are right outside the classroom door, and they do not require any special equipment or materials. Begin with natural objects that are durable and can withstand children's hands. Good leaves for beginners include ash, birch, ginkgo, oak, sassafras, willow, and maple.

Children will find that tempera, fabric, and acrylic paints work well for nature hand printing, as do water-soluble inks. Ink pads are also a good source of paint to be used in nature prints—especially with leaves. Ink pads should not be used with fruits and vegetables because the water-soluble ink will not adhere to a moist surface. If you are nature printing on fabric, be sure to use paint specifically designed to work on cloth;

fabric paint is usually acrylic based. Find a flat area for the work surface. Children can try bristle or soft-hair paintbrushes as well as brayers as they apply the paint or ink to the natural object.

Consider using some of the following natural items for printing:

- Fern leaves
- Maple seed pods
- Seashells
- Cattails
- Pieces of bark
- Starfish
- Gingko leaves
- Twigs
- Lavender flowers and stems

Surfaces that tend to work well for printing include the following:

- Canvas
- Paper

- Fabric
- Cardboard boxes
- Handkerchiefs
- Newsprint
- Terra cotta tiles
- Wood planks
- Ceramic pots

Creative Child Care Center (Charlottetown, Prince Edward, Canada)

Big-Sized Nature Construction

In addition to artwork and nature hand printing, children can also use natural objects such as sticks and branches to construct forts, dramatic-play scenes, and hideaways. These types of authentic structures are a perfect addition to indoor and outdoor environments. With larger projects, children

The Nature Preschool at Irvine Nature Center (Owings Mills, Maryland)

Hunter River Early Learning Center (Charlottetown, Prince Edward, Canada)

Child Development and Learning Laboratory at Central Michigan University (Mount Pleasant, Michigan)

Make a Hideout

by Sharon Lovejoy, author and illustrator

Children love a place of their own to use as a hideout. I once saw a wonderful tepee—a perfect place for summer play.

Here's how to make it: Set four to six poles in the ground at an angle and bring them together at the top, securely lashing them with some heavy twine to form a tepee shape. Run twine roughly around the tepee to form a ladder for scarlet runner beans or showy painted lady beans and varieties of gourds. Plant the seeds all around the base of the tepee.

As the vines begin to reach upward, the children will be fascinated with the climbing process and the searching tendrils. You can explain how some vines always wind clockwise and others always wind counterclockwise.

As the tepee fills in, it becomes a secluded dream and a play-inspiring hideout. An added treat is that the children can use the gourds to make bird houses, bowls, nests, and toys—the possibilities are endless. They will be so proud that they grew the gourds themselves!

often construct over a number of days, change the overall size and shape of the structure, and discover new and more inventive uses for the natural objects as the play evolves.

The most significant reason for constructing with locally found natural materials is the physical connection with the community's topography, flora, and fauna. When children become familiar with their natural

> " Nature teaches us how the world works.
> Imagination teaches us how to dream.
> Play teaches us how to make our dreams real.
> —**Sarah Olmsted,** *Imagine Childhood*

Constructing with pieces of wood.

surroundings, they experience a sense of place and belonging—both critically important in social and emotional growth. Also, the versatility of nature encourages children's creativity. Nothing in nature says to the child "use me this way," so children find self-satisfaction in using these gifts from the earth. Become a witness to children's discoveries and stand in awe. Cherish the opportunity of joining

Children cooking up hay stew.

156

Roadside Treasures

- - - - - - - - - - -

by Kay Koern, avid collector of nature's gems

My Grandma Miesch would have loved Martha Stewart. Driving along the highway, she would tell my grandpa, "Pull over right now!" Garden clippers were kept on the car's floor in the back seat. When Grandpa obediently (but not always happily) pulled over to the side of the road, Grandma would jump out, grab the clippers, and begin cutting and gathering long-stemmed and unusually shaped pods with spikes going in all directions. These priceless finds would later be carefully sorted, dried, spray-painted gold, and then artistically placed into an arrangement to grace her kitchen table. Sometimes they were combined with other dried treasures she had collected from the side of the road to make more elaborate centerpieces.

My grandma taught me about the wonders and beauty of nature. In a quest to preserve nature's bounty, I began looking at everything outside as an opportunity to create something lasting and one of a kind. As I have grown older, I find myself collecting things from nature found at the beach, on the roadside, and in the woods. Often these newfound objects make impromptu table decorations for a dinner party. Sometimes I mix these found objects with flowers from my garden, rocks, shells, ferns, and anything else captivating my imagination.

My own grandchildren have now joined me in hunting and collecting nature's gifts outside—sometimes to make our spring table special or as supplies for a craft. They have learned that we don't need to run to a store to buy decorations, and they take pride in creating unique and beautiful table settings for celebrations with family.

children with nature. Understand how important it is for them to be present and connected to the local community and the earth.

Connecting with Clay

Playing with clay is an ideal way to ground children to the earth's natural energy. When children knead and pound clay with their bare hands, they are connecting to an organic element. This natural connection is important because the lives of today's children are filled with an overabundance of manmade materials. Most teachers, for example, typically stock and use playdough in their classrooms. While some teachers purchase the manufactured Play-doh through an early childhood catalog or at the local store, others make their favorite recipe at home or possibly in the classroom with the children as a learning experience. Although the exact ingredients of Play-doh are proprietary, the commercially purchased mixture is made up of salt, water, and flour (and probably some type of preservative), which is pretty much the same ingredients as the homemade version. Clay, on the other hand, contains natural materials from the earth. When children use natural clay, their hands come in contact with the elements making up the earth, such as rock, soil, and water. Because children use their hands (and sometimes toes and other parts of their bodies) to play with natural clay, the opportunity for grounding

Community Play School (Baltimore, Maryland)

Rethinking the Classroom Landscape

to the earth is monumental. In addition to becoming grounded with a natural element, clay offers many other important learning benefits for young children.

It Is Therapeutic

Young children love clay. It is easy to poke, pull, squeeze, push, and join together. Working with clay can calm children as they manipulate and roll the substance in their hands. Natural clay also can be used over and over again. If properly stored, it can last a very long time. Protect the longevity of clay by placing it in a container with an air-tight lid. Line the container with a plastic kitchen garbage bag to help keep the clay moist. After children have played with the clay, it is important to moisten it. Children can help

by giving the thirsty clay a drink of water. Roll the clay into balls about the size of a small orange and simply spray the balls a few times with water. The clay will then be soft for the next clay play.

It's a Big Idea

Educator Bev Boss had a reputation for urging early childhood practitioners to get rid of the playdough because it is too small for children's big ideas. Commercially purchased Play-doh comes in small containers with each color neatly packed inside. In many preschool classrooms, the small containers are stored in the teacher's cabinet; in other classrooms, the plastic containers of playdough are kept on low shelves with easy accessibility for the children. Regardless of where the containers are stored, the process of removing and returning their clay work to the small containers must be discouraging for children on so many levels.

There is not nearly enough clay in these typically small containers of playdough for children to create their really big ideas. Although playdough can be formed into basic shapes, it is not strong enough to hold much weight upon itself. Natural clay, on

A Potter's Thoughts
- - - - - - - - - - - -

by Jeremy South, clay potter

Kids love the feel of wet clay! Smashing, squeezing, and rolling seem to come naturally to kids as they experience clay. We learn through our hands, so clay is a perfect medium for children's learning. Young children are all about creating; they do not get caught up in working with clay to create a product as adults too often try to do. With children, it's all about the process and has so little to do with the product. As adults, we become so focused on the product that we never really start the process.

We are made of this earth, and young kids inherently have a strong connection to the natural world. As we get older, unfortunately, our own insecurities disconnect us from this reality. Adults can learn a lot from young children and their work with clay.

the other hand, has more vertical stability and can support important artistic details children frequently wish to include in their sculpture work. At the end of clay time (which always feels too short), the children begrudgingly destroy their masterpieces and stuff the playdough back into the small containers. Rather than having children suffer this less-than-desirable experience, many early childhood experts are turning their back on small amounts of clay and turning toward mounds and mounds of clay.

It Makes a Great Center

Consider setting up a clay center just as you would go about setting up a block or home-living area in your classroom. Perhaps the clay center could be a part of your art area. Find a table (for instance, a kitchen table with shortened legs) to hold the clay. You might want to place a piece of granite on the top of the table, which makes a great foundation for clay construction. Go to a local granite shop and ask if they have any remnants that either you could inexpensively purchase or they would donate to a good cause. The granite helps to keep the natural clay cool and moist. You can also use a clay board, which is a board or tray covered in muslin. The larger the working surface, the better. Purchase as much natural clay as you can afford and mound it on the table. Add clay tools such as wood spatulas, spoons, and paddles. Old kitchen utensils work well.

The clay center should be open and available to the children when other centers are accessible. At the end of the day, place a moist towel over the clay mound. Then drape a plastic tablecloth over the entire table. If clay dries out, give it a drink by simply having children make holes like a pot with their pointer fingers, adding water, and pinching the pot together over top of the water. This technique is called pinch pots. Some other tips include the following:

- Position the clay by a water source for easy cleanup of children's hands.
- To keep the clay clean, require children to wash their hands prior to playing at the clay table.
- Position clay away from heat sources and direct sunlight.
- Because the clay never goes away into tiny plastic containers, encourage children to be respectful of others' unfinished work.
- Use wet paper towels to keep children's hands moist while working with the clay.

Adopting a Tree

Find a nearby tree to adopt and love. The tree can be the children's grounding companion. There are plenty of grounding experiences to do with a tree:

- Hug it.
- Do a bark or leaf rubbing.
- Sit under its leafy canopy.
- Read a storybook to children.

- Lean against your tree.
- Observe living creatures who call the tree home.
- Hang a tire swing, and swing from it.
- Feel the different textures of the tree, and then photograph these surfaces.
- Gather its autumn leaves, and toss them into the air like confetti.
- Lie on your back, and watch the leaves flutter in the breeze.
- Sway and move like a tree in a gentle wind, heavy rainstorm, or tornado.
- Listen to the sounds of the tree.
- Move naptime outside, and sleep under the tree's canopy of leaves.
- Measure the tree's diameter using your own body parts, such as hand spans and arm lengths.
- Build an autumn leaf house on the ground near the tree.
- Make a present, and give it to the tree.
- Hang a bird feeder, and lay in the grass to watch the birds.
- Sketch the tree.
- Collect the tree's ground gifts (pods, sticks, buckeyes, leaves), and create a sculpture or mobile.
- Shake its branches, and see what falls to the ground.

When children adopt a nearby tree, they develop an appreciation and awareness of the tree. Children may easily observe, for example, the tree's seasonal

Photo courtesy of Denika Hucks (Killeen, Texas)

changes or the new bird nest in its branches. However, observation is not enough. It is also important for children to connect with the tree through feeling, touching, and physically experiencing the tree's wonder in a close-up, hands-on, and personal way—all without

Long Lake Park (Scotts, Michigan)

manmade barriers such as shoes, socks, or gloves. These rich kinesthetic interactions with the adopted tree promote not only a more enhanced understanding of the individual tree, but a greater connection to the child's own backyard and immediate community.

When children make gifts for the local neighborhood trees, they not only learn respect, but are given opportunities to observe the tree close up when presenting the child-made gifts. Close observation helps children understand the tree's growth cycle and its physical changes. And children's gifts add beauty to the immediately visible part of the world in which they live.

Rethinking the Classroom Landscape

Engaging Children with Nature: More than Just Exposing Them to It

by Eric Strickland, PhD, consultant on issues related to play

The children had invented their own game: hopping from one log to another as they made their way through the nature garden at the child care center. "Don't touch the ground; it's really water and there are sharks everywhere! Yeah . . . if you touch the ground you'll get eaten up."

We're all familiar with these children's games. Whether children are bounding from log to log, hopping from rock to rock, or climbing up and down a playground structure, the story is the same: Children are myopically focused on the process and games of play. If process is the key element in early childhood play, do we really accomplish something better because of the material the children are using? Is play really different or simply better because a manufactured structure rather than a natural element is used? In the example of the shark game, there probably would not be a difference because the children were not actively engaged with nature. Rather, they were merely exposed to it while engaged in the process of doing something else.

The current trend of including more nature and natural elements in early childhood settings has gained considerable traction in recent years and since the publication of *Last Child in the Woods* by Richard Louv. He touched on a feeling we recognized as truth: Children need contact with nature. Much of the intent to reengage children in playing in natural settings has hit the mark, but some—especially equipment manufacturers scrambling to make more-natural equipment—have missed the real intent: To engage children with nature in the process of play. In other words, we don't want simply to expose children to nature or natural elements so we can check off the box on our playground assessment form, but we want children to engage with nature and experience its myriad of details and intricacies.

Tree cookies, a familiar staple of the natural playground movement, are an example of the difference between children's exposure and engagement. Typically, children's exposure to tree cookies includes stacking, hopping, and jumping

(continues)

off. Engagement with and observation of the tree cookies does not occur unless a teacher gives specific directions to do so. Treezles, a unique tree puzzle, may be one way to resolve this challenge. Treezles are different from other wooden puzzles in that the features and characteristics of the tree itself provide the cues for completing the puzzle. In order to solve the puzzle, children must engage with the unique shapes, colors, and patterns on each individual piece as it relates to the whole puzzle.

Treezles are harvested from storm-damaged trees and are hand cut and hand finished to emphasize the natural characteristics of each section of the tree. Because everything of significance that happens to a tree leaves a residual effect, these effects form clues for solving the puzzle. The growth and loss of a branch on a tree creates a collar, which is a slightly raised area at the base of the branch. Each collar has a distinctive shape and pattern. Cutting through the branch collar during preparation of a Treezle forms two mirrored halves that children can match to help complete the puzzle. There are no two trees alike in the universe, and so it is with children and with Treezles.

For more information, visit Eric Strickland's website (http://ericstricklandplaygrounds.com/).

Jumping in Puddles

Sometimes the simplest and most readily available experiences in nature provide the most fun, like jumping in puddles. Water is inherently captivating to children. Children have a primal need to see, hear, and feel water. While jumping in puddles, the water provides many sensory experiences, such as feeling the refreshing water droplets on the face, the solid splash and coolness of the water on the legs, and the exhilaration in the chest.

Jumping in puddles is a way for children to throw their bodies and souls into the serious business of play,

while also learning about cause and effect (jump and you get wet). They experience sensory feedback such as how heavy their socks and pants are when wet or how cold their skin feels when splashed with water. Jumping in puddles is a great exercise to increase endorphins, which act like an antidepressant of sorts and help build immunities. So young children might actually be healthier for jumping through puddles, contrary to what grandma might believe.

Here are a few more quick and easy ideas for connecting to the ground:

- Create a list and have a nature scavenger hunt to look for natural objects.
- Study blades of grass with magnifying glasses to see what creatures might live there.
- Sit in the grass and look for a four-leaf clover.
- Find a big rock, flip it over, and see what's under the rock.
- Plant a garden. Grow child-safe herbs and vegetables, harvest, prepare, and serve as a snack.
- Visit a pumpkin patch, apple orchard, or local garden.
- Make snow angels or build snow people.
- Go on a bird-watching expedition, being sure to bring binoculars, a bird identification chart or book, a clipboard and pencils for documentation, and a camera.
- Look for shadows at various times of the day.
- Pick a bouquet of wildflowers.

Not only should you provide opportunities for children to find joy in connecting to the earth, but it is important for you to join in. So jump in puddles, dig in dirt, and hug a tree.

Knowing Where You Are

In her book *The Goodness of Rain: Developing an Ecological Identity in Young Children*, author Ann Pelo notes that our work as early childhood educators is to invite children to braid their identities together with the place where they live by calling their attention to elements of the natural world, such as the sky, ground, sand, trees, water, and mountains.

(continues on page 178)

The Summer of the Beaver Dam: My Childhood Gift of Appropriate Challenge and Its Influence on My Work Today

by Nancy Rosenow, executive director, Nature Explore

I was fortunate to grow up in the 1960s in a suburb of Philadelphia that had not been overdeveloped at that time. Today, most of the wild places I played in as a child are now high-rise apartments or supermarkets. (More about that later.) I really did experience what many now call a "free-range childhood"—a chance to discover the natural world without a great deal of adult interference. I was blessed to live close to fields full of wildflowers, meandering creeks and streams, and small forest glades. In the summertime, all of those great spaces especially beckoned to the gaggle of children who lived in my neighborhood. We longed to explore. And we did—for hours—in groups of mixed ages, and very often without adult supervision.

Today, if news stories are any indication, parents could be cited for child neglect if they dealt with their children the way our parents did. Many a summer day began early in the morning when they shooed us out the door to go play. Soon, groups of children ranging in age from four to ten headed off on adventures into the forested areas to try our skills at tree climbing, or to the meadow to pick bright blue and buttery yellow flowers, or to the stream, which was one of our favorite destinations. We were often gone for most of the day, and the adults in our lives expected that we'd be fine and that we'd come home for meals. None of us ever got seriously hurt, and if there were some bumps or bruises, we all cared for each other. (More on that later, also.)

What is there about flowing water that fascinates young children? The stream on the edge of my neighborhood was actually fairly large (but not deep) and its current was brisk. One of the older boys in our crew had studied beavers in school and regaled us all with stories of how beaver dams could actually hold back the flow of water. Somehow

(continues)

this became a challenge to all of us that occupied hours of our time throughout long muggy days. Our multiage group decided it would be our goal to build a large enough "beaver dam" to be able to hold back all the water in our stream. It was an exciting challenge and I remember being thrilled to be part of it. (I was one of the youngest and felt honored to be included.)

The summer of the beaver dam lives in my memory as a time of absolute child-initiated learning in the best sense of the word. The project (although we never called it that) lasted a good six weeks and turned a stretch of lazy summer days into an exciting period of exploration, discovery, problem solving, mutual support, social-skill development, and confidence building. It still remains one of my best childhood memories.

It was a fabulous example of providing children with an appropriate amount of risk. I know our parents were not completely oblivious to what we were doing. They knew about the stream and had probably done an informal risk assessment among themselves about the potential dangers balanced against the benefits. They were interested in the stories we had to tell at the dinner table, but they never tried to take over. They sometimes asked if we'd like snacks to take along, and helped us stuff apples and canteens full of water into satchels we slung over our backs. They talked to the older children about watching out for the young ones. The over-arching message they gave all of us was this: We trust you to watch out for yourselves, to be mindful of what you're doing, to take care of each other, and to use your good minds. They never said that in those exact words, but that's what we heard.

Our stream project taught us all about persistence. We thought we could create a dam in a few days, but our first attempts were woefully inadequate. We carried over a few logs and some smaller sticks and plopped them in the water just to watch the flowing stream carry them away. We were flummoxed. When we all talked to our parents about our first failures, they gave us words of encouragement. "Keep trying." And we did. We tried multiple ways of creating dams. The older children decided we needed to build something sturdier and sent the youngest ones to gather leaves and mud. They sent the next-to-oldest to look for larger logs. Although it was slow progress, our dams got closer and closer to working. I remember being so proud when I suggested using pine branches as part of the "glue" to hold things together, and my idea actually helped.

Our beaver-dam summer was full of authentic learning. Nature was an exciting teacher, but a demanding one. We had to be careful when we carried heavy logs, and we had to watch for hornets when we dug up mud. The oldest boy decreed that the "little children" couldn't walk in the stream without holding an older one's hand. Sometimes we argued, often we tried things that just didn't work, but always we learned. I remember, over and over, experiencing the thrill of great effort toward a shared endeavor, and reveling in the sheer exuberance of it all. When we finally built the dam that actually worked, everyone cheered . . . and cheered . . . and cheered.

Fast forward many years later. I've long since moved away from my childhood town, but when I go back to visit I mourn the loss of the wild places. They've all been bulldozed over, and the stream is inaccessible to children. Parents probably would be afraid to allow their youngsters to explore anyway, worried that others would see them as neglectful. In reflecting on this story, I realized how very much my

(continues)

(*Continued*)

summer experiences were a motivator for the work I do today with the Dimensions Educational Research Foundation and our Nature Explore Program, a joint endeavor with the Arbor Day Foundation.

You see, a lot of our work involves bringing that type of beaver-dam experience to where children spend their days: early childhood programs, elementary schools, domestic violence or homeless shelters, children's museums, and libraries. We know that so many of today's children won't get the opportunity to experience the thrill of exploration in nature, filled with appropriate risk and authentic learning, unless we adults re-create some of the experiences that used to happen naturally. Many of the schools we work with in urban areas tell us that their children just don't live close to any wild spaces anymore, and families aren't able to take trips out into nature very often, if ever.

So when our teams work collaboratively with programs to create nature-filled outdoor classrooms outfitted with large areas filled with wood chips, logs, and sticks, I know we are bringing to today's children some of the same thrill of exploration, effort, and problem solving (and yes, a bit of risk) that I experienced as a child.

Last summer, in one of our Certified Nature Explore classrooms, I watched as a group of children of mixed ages worked together over many weeks to figure out how to manipulate bamboo poles into a lean-to structure that would be sturdy enough to stand on its own. I knew that teachers had assessed the risks of this situation and asked the older children to show that they understood how to move the poles around safely without injuring others. They also gave them the same admonishment I heard from my parents many years ago: "Watch out for the younger ones." Teachers were close by and interested if children wanted to talk, but they didn't take over. When the lean-to fell over multiple times, teachers had the same advice my parents gave fifty years ago: "Keep trying."

I only visited occasionally, so I was fortunate to be present on the day that the plan that actually worked was conceived. I was there as all the trial-and-error learning, all the appropriate risk taking, all the problem solving, confidence building, and social-skill development came to fruition as the sturdy structure held and stood on its own. And I watched through my tears as children cheered . . . and cheered . . . and cheered!

The Waterfall

- - - - - - - -

by Liana Chavarin, director, Berkeley Forest School

Three children, ages three, four, and five, watch the waterfall. This creek is one they know. Yet it's not trickling like it was at the start of the school year, and it's not overflowing from the storms like it did a few weeks ago. It is steady, and significant.

Today the children watch together in silence. They watch the water rush down; they observe.

They are calm and content. Teachers do not disturb them. Teachers see the value of their self-directed observation. These children commune with nature, with water, with its power and peace.

They sit silently for a time (much longer than many adults would expect is possible), then get up to leave one by one, without words exchanged. Words aren't necessary.

Berkeley Forest School (Berkeley, California)

The Heart in the River

by Rebecca Kreth

As a young child, I don't remember thinking much about the connection between place and self. I do remember, however, the many wonderful and warm summer hours spent swimming in the river that flows through my family's homestead. Alongside my cousins, we would jump from the rocks, splash each other, and swim in the cool river water. Many years later at a family reunion—for old time's sake—I went swimming with my younger cousin. While laughing,

gliding, and swimming downriver, it occurred to me that I was repeating history in much the same way my parents and grandparents had done with me as a child. When we came to the familiar shallow rapids, I stood up with my head filled with precious childhood memories. My heart swelled with great love for the land on which I stood and the fresh, cool waters swirling around me . . . and immediately

thought, "I should look for a heart rock. It will help me remember this very moment—this heartfelt connection between place and self." The idea seemed hopeless, however, as I looked down at the gazillion rocks beneath my feet. An inner voice said, "Look under your foot," and I realized a small stone was lodged between my toes.

After picking up and examining the stone, I amazingly discovered it was a smooth soft white stone in an almost perfect shape of a heart. There in an instant, the stone spoke to me. In a heartbeat, I was connected to the land and waters of my ancestors and filled with humble gratitude for my family and my heritage. I now carry with me memories like this of who I am and how this river place shaped my young life, and I cherish those thoughts while working with today's young children and their families.

A Family Tradition

by Sandra Duncan

It was a family tradition, a yearly excursion, an adventure, and a lesson in negotiation. Exactly fourteen days before Christmas, my family would pile into the station wagon with the wood panels on its sides and drive to my uncle's pine tree lot to find and chop down the world's most perfect tree. We would tromp around in the Michigan snow looking for the biggest, greenest, tallest, and most beautiful (at least to our eyes) pine tree. It would take hours—and much negotiation—to decide which tree to call our own. My little brother would think he found the most "boo-tee-full" tree, but being the practical big sister, I would say: "Look, it has no branches in the middle so we won't be able to hang any decorations there, and the tree will be ugly." Ever the peacemaker, mom would suggest putting Charley's tree in the corner of the living room so we wouldn't be able to see the bare ugly spot. My dad would simply sigh. Eventually, after much discussion and sometimes crocodile tears, we would all get a turn at helping to chop down this perfect tree.

Once home, Dad would often find that we truly did find the biggest tree on the lot. He would have to trim the boughs so the tree would fit in the house. These bits and pieces of tree boughs became garnishes for our home's holiday décor. Some of the boughs were placed in the middle of the dining room table alongside my mom's antique china for holiday meals. Other pine boughs were placed on the living room's windowsills. But the best and finest pieces were designated for making the front door's wreath. My mom took a wire coat hanger and bent it into a circle to use as a base for the wreath. Dad would use pliers and thin wire to attach the boughs to the coat hanger circle.

Listening to holiday songs on the kitchen's radio, my brother and I would sit at the small wooden table threading (with real sewing needles, of course) raw cranberries on a string, and then we would help mom weave the cranberry strings to decorate the pine-bough wreath. The pièce de résistance was a gigantic red ribbon attached to the wreath's top.

I remember the music; I remember the laughter; I remember the accomplished feeling when the wreath was finally finished. But most of all I remember the poignant delicious smell and the pleasant feel of the pine boughs on my small hands as our family created the most beautiful holiday wreath in the world.

Caring for Chickens

by Ruth Wilson, author and education consultant

By the time I was six years old, I was weeding corn, picking tomatoes, and helping take care of animals on the farm where I grew up. One of my daily chores was watering the chickens. This job involved filling a bucket with water from a spigot by our house and carrying it through the yard and out to the chicken coop. There, I'd pour the water into a long wooden trough. I had to make several trips across the yard to make sure the chickens had enough water throughout the day.

Once I learned to read, I became a book lover and would spend as much time as I could reading books I borrowed from the school or public library in our small hometown of Columbus Grove, Ohio. There were times when I became so engrossed in a book that I would take it with me when I went out to water the chickens. I remember walking through the yard with a bucket of water in one hand and an open book in my other hand. I had found a way to combine my love of reading with doing my chores! Both activities taught me many lessons about life.

Books introduced me to a much wider world than I could experience on a farm or in a small midwestern town. From books, I learned about history, art, and culture. I learned about other places and other peoples. I entered imaginary worlds where hopes and dreams could take many different forms. But I never forgot the chickens.

From the chickens, I learned that animals are not only a source of food but that they also share many things in common with us, as humans. From the moment I held a baby chick in my hand and felt its tiny heart beating, I began to see chickens as living beings—not just as resources existing for our benefit. Once I held a baby chick, watering the chickens became so much more than a daily chore; it became a way of taking care of other living things. Skipping my chores was never an option, as watering the chickens meant more than just doing what I was told or finding a way to keep busy. I knew the chickens would die if they didn't have water.

Baby chicks, I learned, were fragile, requiring very special care and protection. A treasured memory I have from childhood is staying in the chicken coop with my dad during a thunderstorm. Dad explained how thunder and the noise of heavy rain pounding on the tin roof could frighten the baby chicks enough to cause them to panic. Frightened baby chicks, Dad said, tend to huddle together, crushing some of them in the process. We stayed with the chicks until the storm passed. We had a radio and played some music—more for the chickens than for us. We wanted to distract the chicks from the sounds of the storm and keep them calm.

From chickens, I also learned something about interdependence. I saw how some of the grain we grew in the fields was made into feed for the chickens. The chickens, in turn, provided us and others in the community with a daily source of food. I continue to marvel at how plants, animals, and people are all so closely connected in a wondrous web of life.

I know that watering the chickens and staying with them during a storm made a difference for the chickens. I know it made a difference for me, as well. I treasure the lessons I learned from the chickens and appreciate the many ways my early experiences on the farm have helped me become more aware of the wonders of life all around me.

classroom? What do children see on their way to school or the classroom? What is interesting in the immediate neighborhood? What seasonal changes have happened on the playground or beyond the fence? What is in the crack of the sidewalk or between the blades of grass?

Because children live in the present, they see things we don't notice. They are fascinated by found objects or snippets of nature we—as adults—find ordinary.

(*continued from page 168*)

Knowing where you are in the world—what that looks, feels, smells, tastes, and sounds like—helps to define ourselves in relation to the larger world. Children live in the present moment in relationship to every other thing and being. Acknowledging the importance of young children's here-and-now attitude is critical when creating classroom environments. Children are most interested in what is happening right this minute in their lives. So how can you acknowledge children's current and present mind-sets in your classroom?

One strategy is to look outside the classroom door or windows. What do you see from the windows of your

Curious about what is right in front of them or just beneath their feet, young children learn from the here and now.

American psychologist Abraham Maslow recognized young children's propensity for living their lives from moment to moment without thought of the future. Maslow described these moments of childhood as self-actualization and peak experiences, which occur frequently in the lives of young children. These peak experiences are oftentimes missed by even the most observant teacher because they occur in the blink of an eye. Because children are always learning—every time, everywhere, and every moment—it is our prime

A Story of Here and Now

by Mari Potter, lead teacher, Child Development and Learning Laboratory

Just outside Central Michigan University's Child Development and Learning Laboratory, children were intrigued by the large construction site. Observing their interest, the teacher encouraged the children to document the progress of the construction site. The children's photography project evolved into displaying their photographs on an overhead projector in the indoor movement room as well as incorporating building blocks to provide inspiration for constructing their own buildings. The project brought a familiar part of the outside community into their everyday school community.

Central Michigan Child Development and Learning Laboratory (Mount Pleasant, Michigan)

responsibility to recognize and honor the immediacy of children's peak experiences through our classroom environments. Our classrooms must be appropriately designed and ready to support young children's self-actualizations. This means our environments must be flexible, quickly altered, and in continuous alignment with this very moment of childhood. We must be in the here and now of our children, their families, and community. We must link our classrooms to the geography, topography, flora, and fauna of children's immediate community and neighborhood—the here and now.

Strategies for Linking Your Classroom to the Topography

Even though there are common elements (tables, chairs, bookshelves, and equipment) found in most classrooms, many of these elements do not reflect the community, industry, geography, flora, and fauna surrounding the facility. The way in which you enrich these common elements could be quite different based on the topography and landscapes surrounding you. A science center in the mountain regions might be very different from one in the coastal regions. In the mountain region, for example, the teacher may enrich the science center with pinecones and red rocks. Whereas, the science center in the coastal regions

may be enhanced with sand and seashells. In Alaska, where birchwood trees are abundant, the sensory table might be filled with the tree's beautiful and luscious-feeling bark.

Encourage Activities Using Natural Materials

Andy Goldsworthy, a British sculptor, photographer, and environmentalist, can be found on most days in the forest near his home in Penpont, Scotland. Goldsworthy is a brilliant artist who uses nature as his canvas to create works of awe-inspiring beauty. Much of his environmental artistry is ephemeral, which means it is made to disappear or perhaps be transformed and altered by human passersby or even forest creatures.

Goldsworthy's environmental art celebrates personal engagement with the natural world. During a warm spring rain, for example, Goldsworthy was once found lying on a rock with his arms and legs stretched out waiting for the drizzling water to create an outline of his body on the rock's surface. When the rain stopped and the sun came out, Goldsworthy photographed his disappearing shadow as it evaporated. He once made a 7-foot chain of red poppies that stayed stuck together with saliva long enough for a photograph to be taken before the wind carried the poppies away. Goldsworthy's art tools are his hands, and his art is made from found objects, such as the quill of a feather, a sharp stone, or a stick. His work involves making intimate connections with nature by finding, touching, and placing natural items.

Unlike Goldsworthy, today's young children are increasingly disconnected from their immediate outside world, the community's flora and fauna, and its topography. Many children have limited opportunities for creative expression and collaborative action (working together as a group toward a common goal). Connect children with their community's landscapes by providing experiences to work and collaborate together with local natural resources. Try some of the following ideas.

Rock balancing. In many neighborhoods, rocks are plentiful and easily accessible in the local landscape. If you are fortunate enough to live in such a community, engage children in the experience of rock balancing.

Making balanced rock sculptures is an art form. Working collaboratively or independently, children can explore their creativity, use problem-solving skills, and develop their self-expression. Rock balancing is also an exploration of the forces of gravity as well as other laws of physics. Invite children to personally engage with nature as they create magnificent rock towers, sculptures, and beautiful works of art.

Beach art. If you are lucky enough to be near the water, celebrate by creating art on the beach using sand, shells, seaweed, and other beach treasures. Connect with nature by creating sandcastles or spirals from seashells. Children become environmental artists as they create seaweed dragons stomping through a forest of driftwood trees and sea-washed rocks. Invite parents and community members to join in and become contributing artists. And by the next daybreak, the lapping waves may change or completely wash away the children's artwork.

Tree cookies. In many areas of the United States, trees are part of the community's local landscape and are an easily accessible natural resource. The many parts of the tree (twigs, stumps, bark, leaves, and pinecones) can be used in a multitude of ways in

A tree cookie is a slice of a lovely tree trunk. Just about any diameter will work, and they are usually from 1 to 10 inches thick. Anything thicker could be classified as log seating, as in a wooden stool. If you have a tree that needs to be trimmed or cut down, you can use an electric or manual saw to slice the branches or trunk pieces to a uniform thickness. It is best to make the edges as even as possible. You can also find

Downtown Baltimore Child Development Center (Baltimore, Maryland)

the early childhood classroom. So look outside and see what kinds of trees are in your backyard, in the neighborhood park, or on the playground. Think about how you could incorporate the tree topography of your neighborhood into the classroom. One way is to include tree cookies inside and outside.

these delightful tree cookies through nature-based learning catalogs, at your local lumberyard, or possibly through local tree cutters and forestry operations units.

If the tree cookies have rough edges from the sawing process, you can use sandpaper to smooth out the edges. This is a perfect project for older children. You can also put a coat of shellac on the tree cookies. However, doing this blocks the earthy smell of some woods and eliminates the kinesthetic experience children get by touching the wood's texture. To ensure that the tree cookies are insect-free, bake them on a low temperature for about fifteen minutes.

Children of all ages find tree cookies to be endlessly fun and forever useful. Very young children enjoy picking them up, doing heavy work, and distributing the pieces throughout the indoor and outdoor classroom spaces. Tree cookies can be walked on, hopped on, stacked up, spread out, sat upon, stood upon, and rolled about! They can act as plates, serving platters, bridge pieces, stepping stones, space dividers, plant stands, circle time sit spots, or any other creatively inspired element you can imagine!

Tree cookies are low cost, easily accessible, and terrifically creative elements, especially when you

A Young Boy's Magic Stones

by Dexter Lane, Nature Explore consultant

As we age, we usually forget most details of the magical world we all inhabited when we were very young. As we gradually learn what things are and how they interact, our imagined world fades into a misty past. Our relationships with young children remind us of those early imaginative days.

Nature Explore Outdoor Classrooms, with their abundance of natural materials, offer children the richest stage for imaginative play and many opportunities for adults and children to connect on a level of shared excitement and learning. At Nature Explore, we say that children's connections with nature lead to transformations—in the children, in their schools, and in their families. One such transformation occurred when a young boy's stone collection dissolved a distance between him and his mother, and it also dissolved a distance between her adult self and the child within.

One day an upset mother approached Charlotte, who was the director of a Nature Explore classroom, and said, "Johnny has been bringing home rocks in his pocket and they are going through the washing machine! I have told him he cannot collect rocks anymore!" The director replied, "Have you ever asked him about the stones he is collecting? He is so thoughtful about which ones he selects." Mom replied, "I have just told him he can't collect these anymore. I want you to tell him the same thing." Charlotte knew this was not the teachable moment.

Over the weekend, at a garage sale, Charlotte found a small pill sorter box with multiple compartments, and bought it for a nickel. On Monday she gave it to Johnny, asking him to put his stones in the box instead of his pockets. All week long Johnny thoughtfully added colorful stones to the box—sometimes replacing previously collected ones to refine his collection. On Friday, Charlotte sent home the activity sheet for the Nature Explore Families' Club called "What Is Beautiful to You?" This is an activity that gets the parent and child outside to look for one natural item that is beautiful to each. Johnny took home his container of stones along with the activity sheet.

(continues)

On Monday morning, bright and early, Johnny's mother was back at school. "Oh my goodness, I had no idea the beauty that Johnny was seeing in those stones! He held up one and said, 'Look, Mom, this rock is the color of my favorite shirt!' He held up the next and said, 'Look, Mom, this one has the letter J in it, just like in my name!' He held up one more rock and said, 'Mom, when you look through this one you can see a rainbow!!!'" She paused and said, "I just never knew."

Johnny and his mother began collecting stones together, and proudly displayed them at home. From that day on, there was a transformation between parent and child. In understanding the creative ways Johnny was moved by objects that most adults would pass by, his mother was validating his very personal excitement about learning. Her transformation in attitude from misunderstanding and unintentional rejection to understanding and embracing Johnny's passion created a bond based on shared learning. Johnny's mother also likely experienced connections with her own distant learning experiences, allowing her to participate more fully with her son while collecting stones. What environment offers more numerous, varied, and creative learning

opportunities for children than they can discover in nature? Spending time in nature opens doors to children's rich world of learning—yours, too.

use trees indigenous to your area. When children get practice identifying the tree through the sight, touch, and smell of a tree cookie, they can become acquainted with their neighborhood's immediate landscape.

Infuse the Space with Flowers, Plants, and Trees

Link the community's topography to your classroom by infusing the space with flora and fauna from your surrounding neighborhood. If your classroom, for example, is near a forest—then bring the woodland into your environment. Sound too difficult? It may be easier than you think. Central Michigan University's Child Development and Learning Laboratory decided to honor the trees, woods, and forests surrounding the facility. They named each room after an indigenous tree and installed a wall of that type of wood in corresponding classrooms.

Child Development and Learning Laboratory at Central Michigan University (Mount Pleasant, Michigan)

Above and below: Child Development and Learning Laboratory at Central Michigan University (Mount Pleasant, Michigan)

Dimensions Education Programs (Lincoln, Nebraska)

One of the walls in each of the rooms named after trees is paneled with the corresponding wood. For example, the pine room has a wall of pinewood. Also, the pine room is an area adorned with artificial pine trees.

Even some of the furnishings have evidence of the community's trees, such as the leaf cut-outs in the room dividers. And the center's foyer is also filled with items connected to the topography, flora, and fauna of the neighboring community. Note the tree cookie flooring in the living area and children's artwork made

with locally found autumn leaves that is featured in the harvest display.

Another example of linking the community's topography, flora, and fauna is the Downtown Baltimore Child Development Center. Located near a major seaport, this center recognized the city's waterfront and shipping industry by painting a mural on the back wall of the center's library. Even the sign for the center hints of the seaport, with its nautical-looking lettering.

Throughout the center, there are other reflections of the community, such as a mural showing the Maryland state flower, the black-eyed Susan, and decorations using seashells that are hung overhead for children to see and enjoy.

To replicate the nearby Michigan forest and the community's habitat at the Children's Discovery Museum, a woodland scene was painted on a large piece of muslin and hung as a theater curtain for

Kids 'N' Stuff (Albion, Michigan)

What We Had Was Trees

– – – – – – – – – – – – – – –

by Dana Wiser, Community Playthings design manager

In 1947, Macedonia Cooperative Community had 800 acres of woodland. The pacifist commune in the Appalachian hills of north Georgia was as poor as the used-up soil, so the question was how could you change trees to dollars? Maybe with persimmon pies? And beanbags called Percy the Pig made from the seed? Maybe with poles from paper pulp? Hassocks inspired by Frank Lloyd Wright?

Everything failed. When the breakthrough came, it was nearly missed—it was just a silver lining. The visitor who took the persimmon pies to sell wasn't heard from again, but he left behind something of far greater value. A former teacher at Caroline Pratt's City and Country School, he shared the dimensions of blocks that could be used for play. The community's bootstrappers used those dimensions to create the Unit Block, and Community Playthings was born.

I am seven years younger than Community Playthings, so it was my older siblings who play-tested the first wooden products. I grew up alongside Hollow Blocks and the Variplay Triangle Set that our logo still features. Love of wood came as naturally as the clear branch water flowing under our footbridge, as naturally as the mountain air.

Woodworking skills came at a high price. Early blocks were of pine, too soft. Poplar did OK until northern red maple came along. The first precious load of dimension stock was spoiled for insufficient dry kiln time. My parents and their fellow co-op pioneers had so much to learn. The going sawmill wage was 10 cents an hour, more than they made cutting and stacking pulp poles by hand. So the order for $2,000 in Unit Blocks from Hawaii public schools earned them credit for machines, and put them on the map.

Playing with wooden trucks morphed seamlessly into making them. Homemade birdhouses preceded dovetail joinery. We always had wood around—and stories about wood. There was treasure hidden in a load of maple from the mill, overlooked bird's-eye or curly maple, the rare board of cherry or black walnut, each piece cherished for its special characteristics and for the new skills and processes it called for. If you hand-sanded long enough, you were rewarded with a deep glow in the finished cherry. Oak, with its open grain, finished with wiped filler.

Working alongside Dad, there were always the stories about learning to make a living with wood. There was the time he visited the U.S. Forest Products Laboratory in Madison, Wisconsin, for advice about woodworking machines. Sixty years later, I found myself there, too, following in his footsteps, to learn about the right wood to use for what became Community Playthings Outlast products. Still so much to learn.

Chippewa Nature Center's Nature Preschool (Midland, Michigan)

dramatic play. Hallways are named after flora such as Elm Expressway, Sassafras Pass, and Ash Alley.

The farming industry is a large part of the local community where Chippewa Nature Center's Nature Preschool is located. There are acres of commercial crops such as cucumbers, corn, and tomatoes. Orchards laden with apples, peaches, and cherries make up the northern Michigan landscape. Green grocers, farm stands, and the farmer's market are peppered throughout the community—especially in the height of the growing season. To recognize this important landscape, picture blocks representing the farmers and their land were created.

Creative Child Care (Charlottetown, Prince Edward, Canada)

Dimensions Education Programs (Lincoln, Nebraska)

In Canada where the Birchwood trees are abundant and fill the landscape, Creative Child Care built an outside play hut made out of natural materials from the local landscape—a place where children gather, sing songs, and roast hot dogs over the pretend camp stove.

Flagstone makes a great base for construction or engineering. You can usually find it at a local garden shop. Look for a piece that has a fairly level surface. Place it on the floor in the block or manipulative corner.

Below, a container filled with birchwood and other types of tree bark infuses the outside local landscape into an early childhood classroom. With all its natural beauty and intricacies, the bark adds visual interest for young children to enjoy.

While on a walk, children collected bits and pieces of pine boughs. They inserted their found treasures into a cork with a premade hole and added liquid glue. While in the block corner, the children can enjoy playing with the miniature trees made from the neighborhood landscape.

Rethinking the Classroom Landscape

Into the Woods

- - - - - - - - -

by Sue Penix, infant and toddler specialist, Baltimore City Child Care Resource Center

During my childhood, I was fortunate enough to be able to experience nature and the great outdoors on a regular basis. This was not always easy for my family to do, as we lived in the city and relied on public transportation. But it was important to my parents that we had the opportunity. So we would walk to a local park or take the bus to begin our adventures in the wild. We were encouraged not to leave any stone or log unturned in search of salamanders, bugs, and worms. We would climb trees and wade in streams. Some of my fondest memories are of building fairy houses at the base of trees from loose parts found in the woods or park we were visiting.

As an educator, I am an avid believer that children should be able to engage in the same types of experiences I had as a child. This became apparent to me when I was sharing information about woodland animals with a group of inner-city children. During the presentation, one of the children asked me where I got all of my "stuff." My stuff was actual artifacts from the woods that I brought into the classroom for the children to explore. I answered, "In the woods." He then asked, "What is *the woods*?" After sharing a story and some photos, he had a better understanding of *the woods*. He then asked, "Can I go to the woods?" My response was a resounding "Yes," and I promptly made arrangements for a trip to a local park.

The children were given permission to turn over stones and logs, to use their magnifying glasses, and to gather loose parts along the way for further exploration. At the end of the trip, the child who asked if he could go to the woods was all smiles. He couldn't wait to share with his mom and dad all of the artifacts he had found there.

Autumn Leaf Project by the Children at Nancy W. Darden Child Development Center (Greenville, North Carolina)

What Experience Do Children Have with Earthing?

Use this questionnaire to determine the level of children's grounding experiences, which helps children connect to the earth and their local community's topography, flora, and fauna.

Directions: Select *A*, *B*, or *C* for each item listed below.

A = Strongly Agree

B = Agree

C = Strongly Disagree

_____ 1. Children are outside at least twice a day—every day.

_____ 2. Children are allowed to play barefoot in the rain and experience mud puddles.

_____ 3. Children are provided opportunities for mud play at least three times a year.

_____ 4. Children physically interact with a variety of natural elements (such as pinecones, seashells, rocks, and sticks) in the classroom at least twice a day—every day.

_____ 5. Natural clay is easily accessible on a daily basis to children.

_____ 6. Water play is offered in the classroom at least once a week—every week.

_____ 7. Water or snow play is offered outside at least once a month—every month.

_____ 8. A variety of natural elements (such as tree cookies, pine boughs, and rocks) reflecting your community's habitat are included and frequently changed in the block area.

_____ 9. A variety of natural elements (such as buckeyes, seashells, and tree bark) reflecting your community's habitat are included and frequently changed in the science area.

_____ 10. A variety of natural elements (such as acorns, pinecones, and sea glass) reflecting your community's habitat are used for counters and game pieces in the math and manipulative centers.

_____ 11. At least one tree stump or branch is in the classroom.

_____ 12. At least three different types of live plants are in the classroom.

_____ 13. At least one living creature (such as fish, a hermit crab, a snake, worms, and a bunny) is in the classroom.

_____ 14. Children have opportunities to participate in both outdoor and indoor gardening experiences and caring for living plants and animals on a regular basis.

Scoring:

This tool helps assess the level of your children's earthing experiences. Remember that the commitment to earthing and grounding is an ongoing process of learning, so there are no correct answers.

If you responded frequently with an *A*, you are well on your way to providing experiences to help children get grounded to the earth's energy, feel more connected, and experience less stress.

If you responded frequently with a *B*, you may need some additional grounding experiences in your classroom environment and provide more opportunities for children to connect with nature and the earth.

If you responded frequently with a *C*, you may want to consider implementing some of the ideas in this chapter by offering natural materials and experiences every day.

5

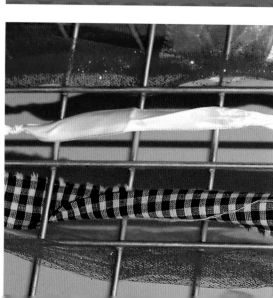

Creating Connected Classrooms: Past and Present

Lend me the stone strength of the past and I will lend you
The wings of the future, for I have them.

—Robinson Jeffers, "To the Rock That Will Be a Cornerstone of the House"

All Things Are Connected

The early childhood classroom is an essential thread in the web of young children's lives. It connects children's outside worlds—primarily their homes and families—with the inside world of the classroom environment. Effectively linking children to your classroom requires keen understandings about their outside worlds. Having insights and knowledge about children's heritages and backgrounds allows you to better develop learning spaces representing each individual and unique child. Using photos, materials, and objects of meaning related to children's families, pets, homes, and neighborhoods, you can design environments where children easily transition from their outside worlds to the inside world of the classroom. To learn more about the lives of children in your classroom, you might distribute a short questionnaire asking families to share information about their cultural history, length of time in the community, favorite foods, and important traditions. By asking families to contribute, you send a message about how much you value their backgrounds.

Invite parents, grandparents, and extended family members to share their heritages through stories, skills, and knowledge in ways that are meaningful to young children. Through real-life demonstrations such as cooking, gardening, whittling, quilting, weaving, and woodworking, children learn about others.

Develop relationships with members of your local city service clubs and recreational leaders. These individuals possess a wealth of knowledge about your community to bring into the classroom.

Contact your city's government to discover the historical background of the land on which your classroom is located. Learn about the heritage of the people who first inhabited the land. Should there be tribal offices in your area, you may be able to connect with the tribal history department to find someone who is available to share stories about historical events.

Connect with organizations or people who have knowledge and understandings of the local land such as a master gardener's club, a county agriculture organization, a park ranger, an environmentalist, or a geologist.

Find elders who are knowledgeable about the community's history. They can support community connections by becoming regular visitors to your classroom.

Linking your classroom to the community engages children's minds and hearts and helps illuminate the understanding of others. Children form deeper and lasting relationships and begin to understand how all things are connected.

Connecting the Past to the Present

Local knowledge is not only connected to the past, but it is also connected to the current as well as future situations. Local or indigenous knowledge is learned (from others and personal experiences) and is continuously adapted according to changing environments. Typically, local knowledge is about subsistence such as tools for hunting, agriculture, and fishing. Closely connected to people's cultural values or need to know for survival, this knowledge is often passed down from generation to generation. A wayfaring sailor, for example, may rely on a nearby fisherman's knowledge about tide times and shoals for safe passage to shore. A fisherman may rely on knowledge from his elders about how to construct strong fishing nets and sturdy boats able to stand up to the salty and treacherous seas. A chef new to the area may rely on local residents' knowledge about which fish are poisonous and which make delicious eating when cooked. In today's fast-paced and ever-evolving world, however, many traditional and culturally or geographically connected knowledge systems are at risk of becoming extinct. As educators of young children, we can shine a bright light on the past and bring some of the community's local knowledge,

which is so close to extinction, into the early childhood classroom.

Traditional Arts

Traditional or folk art is a reflection of life, of community, and of the people's culture. Traditional arts are learned from someone who shares commonalities such as language, ethnic heritage, tribal affiliation, family background, religion, or geographical proximity. These skills are learned behaviors transferred through observations or demonstrations and conversations or word of mouth; following examples illustrated within a particular culture group; and the passing down of elders' or family members' knowledge through generation after generation. Knowledge of traditional arts is a cumulative body of understandings, practices, and know-how developed by peoples with extended histories in the natural environment. Examples of traditional or folk art include the following:

- Basket making
- Wooden boat and canoe building
- Wood carving and whittling
- Step and folk dancing
- Quilting and rag-rug hooking
- Textile weaving
- Flower pressing
- Fly-tying

- Instrument and music making
- Embroidering and knitting
- Pottery making
- Painting and sculpting
- Net making
- Folklore, storytelling, and poetry gathering Wheat weaving
- Drumming
- Mask making

Although countless forms and types of traditional or folk art can be found, interest in maintaining these historical traditions is dwindling. Mass communications and new technologies are penetrating even the remotest communities in the United States, leaving behind a "cultural gray-out and sense of sameness," according to *The Changing Faces of Tradition: A Report on the Folk and Traditional Arts in the United States,* written by traditional arts consultant Elizabeth Peterson. Many people are feeling a loss of community and connectedness. We live in similar-type housing, watch the same television shows, eat at the same restaurants, and shop at the same stores resembling a type of cookie-cutter life experiences. Although we may hold some values in common, we are no longer tied to each other through what Peterson calls practices of commitment. According to Peterson, the visible acts of people's commitments (making, doing, and participating) are missing, which results in

Hope's Home (Prince Albert, Canada)

communities with eroding legacies and a path toward a homogenous society.

Traditional arts celebrate and honor deeply rooted cultural expressions such as music, dance,

never-before-experienced materials. It's about creating something with your hands and not using an electrical plug. It's about collaborating with others and inventing something truly unique—totally unlike anything ever done before. It's about eliciting precious memories and interesting stories to share for generations to come.

Quilt Making

Quilting is often a part of our personal history and heritage. For those of us who grew up hearing stories of relatives who made quilts, these carefully crafted pieces of fabric represent love, care, memories, hope,

crafts, rituals, and stories passed on through families, communities, and tribal, ethnic, and regional groups. These cultural treasures play an important role by expanding awareness and appreciation for the richness of America's heritage and celebrate what we have in common, not what separates us. Traditional arts define us as a people and represent continuity from the past to the present. For young children who live in the here and now, however, participating in traditional arts is not about understanding the connection between the past and the present. Instead, the making, doing, and participating in traditional arts is about storytelling. It's about having experiences with unique and perhaps

> " The hand is the brain's connection to the world around us. In today's world, there is a great deal of concern about children's development of fine motor skills. As our culture moves to being greatly screen-based, we are struggling with how to help the children in our classes who have poor fine motor skills and motor planning. We have to engage children with materials that require fine movements and encourage them to use the mind and the hand simultaneously.
> —**Aimee Fagan,** *Sewing in the Montessori Classroom*

City Neighbors (Baltimore, Maryland)

and creativity expressed through the patterns, materials, and hands of their makers. As interest in exploring family heritage has grown, quilting has revived and blossomed into a creative art form.

Throughout history, people have enjoyed quilts for various reasons. Quilts of course provide warmth and beauty, but they also provide clues to the past. The way a quilt is made can tell the story of its maker, an event, or even an expression of a culture or belief system. Rather than a traditional story told with words, the quilt's story is conveyed through the melding of fabric and stitches. Signature or friendship quilts, for example, were made to remember and honor family members or friends. If a loved one moved away or wasn't able to return home, these quilts served as precious remembrances for those families who had only occasional letters to connect them with friends and relatives back home.

Quilts often tell a story about a person, place, or event in time, which connects those in the past who created the quilt with those in the present who enjoy the beauty of the quilt. No matter what type of quilt is being created, one thing is for sure: adults get enjoyment from working with colors, patterns, and textures that are meaningful to them. Introducing quilt making in the classroom provides similar opportunities for children to enjoy these tactile elements.

There are many ways to introduce the traditional art of quilt making into the classroom. If you are fortunate enough to have a professional quilt maker in the community, plan a behind-the-scenes visit, so children can learn about the process of putting together a quilt. Another idea is to find relatives or friends who will show their beautifully crafted work and explain how quilts are constructed. To find others interested in quilt making, check with your community's historical society, a local 4-H club, quilters' guilds, or commercial hobby stores. Introducing the topic of quilt making with images is a good way to pique children's curiosities. You should be able to find some colorful images on the Internet. If you are a beginner and want to gather information before you introduce the topic to children, you may find these resource books useful:

- *Storybook Quilting* by Jennifer L. Baker and Laurie E. Mehalko
- *Quilt It with Love: The Project Linus Story* by Mary Balagna and Carol Babbitt
- *Sewing in the Montessori Classroom: A Practical Life Curriculum* by Aimee Fagan
- *Show Me How: Quilting: Quilting Storybook and How-to-Quilt Instructions* by Susan Levin and Gloria Tracy

Alexander Graham Bell Montessori School (Wheeling, Illinois)

Classroom quilts can be constructed with many different types of materials, such as fabric or paper of various colors, patterns, and textures. Ask each child to find an interesting piece of paper or fabric to design with markers, paint, or crayons. After gathering and designing their individual square pieces, encourage children to assemble the pieces into a quilt shape using glue, taping, or sewing with thread. Much thought, conversation, and negotiation between the children goes into this phase of the project! Once the children have completed the quilt, display it in a welcoming area where families can enjoy seeing the children's creativity.

Collaboratively made quilts represent individuality as well a sense of community. They reinforce children's collaboration and cooperation, stress equality and uniqueness, and remind children how important it is to accept others' contributions. Continuing to display the works of children who have graduated and gone on to elementary school connects the past to the present in a visually beautiful way.

Flower Pressing

Flower pressing is a traditional art that children and adults can enjoy. Collecting wildflowers is an enchanting way to spend a lazy summer afternoon. And flower pressing does not have to stop with wildflowers. Grasses, leaves, and sea pods are fun to pick, dry, and arrange into bouquets; mix up into potpourri; or artfully affix to an artist's canvas. To dry and press flowers, simply lay them on a paper towel, cover them with another paper towel, and place a heavy book on top. It takes about two weeks to thoroughly press and dry the flowers. There are all sorts of projects children can create with the pressed flowers. Using dried wildflowers, scraps of fabric or paper, or lacy doilies, young children can turn a simple cardboard box into a beautiful work of art. Or dried wildflowers glued to trays, plates, and picture frames can also brighten up a classroom. Create pressed flower cards or pictures by placing

the flowers centrally on the cardboard and carefully dabbing glue under the flower petals. It's fun to find an old straw hat at a resale shop, and transform it into an object of beauty when wildflowers and other natural objects are added to the brim. You can display the children's flower hat in the home-living or dress-up area. You can also decorate a lampshade or picture frame with delicate pressed wildflowers. Another possibility is to make bookmarks or gift tags with the pressed flowers.

Instead of pressing wildflowers, you can try drying them. For ultimate success, pick the fresh flowers on a warm and sunny day. It is best to pick them just before they are in full bloom because the petals are more secure to the stem. To encourage the flowers to dry quickly, remove some of the leaves from the stems. Gather about five medium-sized flower heads and stems and tie them loosely with string. Hang the flower bouquet upside down in a dry and airy room—near the ceiling if possible. Or suspending the flowers from a clothesline draped across the home-living area can provide a wonderful visual reminder of the project. Keep the flowers in this upside down position until they are completely dry, which means they will be brittle to touch. Creating with dried flowers is a delicate business (unless you are making potpourri), so they provide a good lesson in patience and gentle handling for young children.

Weaving

For centuries, weaving played a significant part in American history. The traditional art of weaving included hand-woven rugs, blankets, and clothing. Although some articles, such as rugs, were hand braided, most household items were constructed on a weaving loom.

You can bring back the traditional art of weaving by offering children opportunities to create not only with a wide variety of materials (such as raffia, yarn, rope, pipe cleaners, and ribbons) but also with many different types of weaving bases, such as the following:

- Weaving loom
- Fence
- Strawberry basket
- Mesh kitchen bag
- Picture frame
- Pot holder frames
- Chicken wire
- Place mat with holes
- Colander
- Baking rack
- Onion bag

Child Development and Learning Laboratory at Central Michigan University (Mount Pleasant, Michigan)

Rethinking the Classroom Landscape

Consider some of the following ideas for extending children's weaving activities:

- Invite children to enhance their weavings by bringing in artifacts from home such as photographs, beads, jewelry, feathers, or buttons.

- Encourage families to create weaving projects and share with the classroom.
- Set up a weaving loom or weaving base near the classroom entry. Provide a variety of weaving materials and invite families to explore the various weaving textures and participate in a community weaving project.

Basket Weaving

The art of basket weaving for many cultures, such as Native American people, is a traditional practice. In addition to using baskets in functional ways, such as for storing or carrying goods, you can display them to serve as historical and artistic expressions of the culture, especially indigenous cultures around the world. Using local wild materials found in natural surroundings, basket weaving is a great example of traditional art.

Historically, the process of weaving begins with a relationship with the natural world as well as knowledge of indigenous plants and their life cycles. It is the weaver's time, patience, and value for the craft that goes into the making of each unique and beautiful basket. To the weaver, the process is just as important as the basket itself. Each weaver brings her own set of knowledge and skills to the making of the basket, which then becomes a unique expression and reflection of the weaver. Because young children from any culture enjoy tactile experiences, they are inherently natural weavers. The following information will help you introduce basket weaving in your early childhood classroom.

These materials provide interesting possibilities for basket weaving:

- Rope
- Grasses
- Cord
- Paper
- Raffia
- Vines
- Reeds
- Birch bark
- Sea grass
- Tree branches
- Balsam
- Bamboo
- Twine
- Cardboard
- Newspaper
- Palm leaves

One of the skills of basket weaving is mastering the weaving technique—under, over, and through. So begin young children's basket weaving explorations with simple projects such as making a basket from paper. This material is easy to manipulate, yet the results are traditional looking.

1. Start by cutting strips of construction paper ½ inch wide by 14 inches long. Using two different colors gives the basket a checkered effect. Weave a base of eight to twelve strips by eight to twelve strips, weaving over one and under the next one.

2. The result should resemble a square. The horizontal spokes are one color and the vertical spokes are another color. Your square becomes a woven base of four sides, and each side has one color extending from the base.

3. Gather all the spokes of one color together, and adjust them so that the sides are wide at the bottom and then come together at the top. Glue or staple to secure the ends together. Repeat this for the other three sides.

Photos courtesy of Nicole Louise

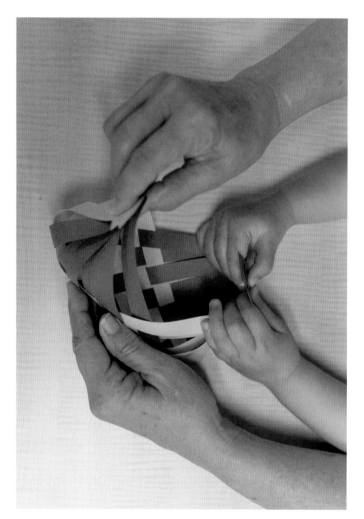

Photos courtesy of Nicole Louise

4. Pull one group of one color together with one group of the other color, and secure them together. Do the same for the other two sections. The wide part is the bottom of the basket, and the pieces come together to create the sides of the basket.

5. Take four more strips of paper (two of each color), and attach them to the sides at opposite corners to make a handle. Children can fill their baskets with their favorite things, such as spring flower blossoms or colorful autumn leaves.

Wreath Making

Wreaths have played an important role in the tapestries of our lives. In ancient history, wreaths were worn as headdresses and were a symbol of power. Head wreaths made from local tree branches and olive leaves became prizes during the Greek Olympics. Almost every ancient culture worshipped nature and its elements as symbols of divine energy so they made wreaths or headdresses from holly, mistletoe, and berries. A symbol of royalty, kings' and queens' crowns began as wreaths made of freshly harvested laurel or lavender. Precious jewels and metals were eventually added to become the crowns we have come to associate with royalty. In the 1960s, the flower child wore wildflower wreaths in her hair to symbolize freedom of spirit. Today's bride often wears a wreath or ring of baby's breath on her head to represent new beginnings. Because the circle symbolizes eternity, the wreath became a fitting addition to funerals. Almost all of us place a wreath (sometimes real—sometimes not) on our front door or the fireplace mantel during the holiday season to symbolize this most joyous time of year.

Wreaths are symbols and representations of life—they represent culture, community, and spiritual, historical, and family traditions. Traditionally, wreaths have been handmade with natural elements from the earth interlaced and woven together. Wreaths reflect the maker's community because the materials used

are typically from the local neighborhood or personal collections. Wreaths also reflect the creator's creative style and personality. They are unique—each one of its own kind, and never duplicated. Wreaths can be a collaborative effort with many individual contributions and efforts, or can be made by a single artisan.

Children experience many benefits when they are given opportunities for wreath making in the classroom. When using natural materials to make wreaths, children become grounded with the earth's elements. As children collaborate to make classroom wreaths, they experience a sense of community and learn how to negotiate when their ideas differ. The children also enjoy kinesthetic experiences as they use their hands to make traditional wreaths.

Use your creativity when selecting a base for classroom wreaths. Although you could purchase a base from the local craft store, consider other less expensive ideas. You could, for example, look around your house for something to use, scour a garage sale, or even create the base by hand. Because some bases are made of natural materials such as moss, dried corn husks, grapevines, or twigs, they are fairly simple to make. You could use a coat hanger or possibly a piece of heavy cardboard as the base. Whatever you choose, be sure the wreath's base will hold up to the weight of the materials you use. Remember, wreaths do not have to be circular; they can be square or rectangular-shaped.

Could you use a picture frame as the wreath's base or perhaps a baking rack or piece of Styrofoam cut to size? A smaller-sized base is easier to handle and works best for young children's hands.

Useful tools for wreath making include a hot glue gun (used with adult assistance), thin floral wire and tapes, white glue, and paper clips or straight pins. Twist-ties from bread wrappers also come in handy when putting the wreath together. You might try some of the following natural materials when making a wreath:

- Dried flowers
- Grasses
- Seeds
- Plants
- Vines
- Dried apples
- Sea glass
- Gourds
- Eucalyptus
- Rose petals
- Seed pods
- Palms
- Cinnamon sticks
- Dried oranges
- Bean pods
- Leaves
- Moss
- Seashells
- River rocks
- Bittersweet
- Dried herbs
- Buckeyes
- Rose hips
- Twigs
- Corn husks
- Coral
- Nuts
- Fresh basil
- Bay leaves
- Holly berries
- Whole nutmeg
- Lavender sprigs

- Yucca
- Sweet gum
- Pinecones
- Rosemary stalks
- Evergreens
- Rocks
- Tree bark

- Cloves
- Lentils
- Acorns
- Ferns
- Pussy willows
- Wisteria
- Pine needles

Tools

A tool is defined as anything that can be used to help get something accomplished. Many of the tools we use today trace back to the sharpened stones called flints that early man created. Used for hunting, fishing, and daily activities, flints were versatile life-saving tools.

Stone was an often-used material for making tools needed to be long-wearing (such as hammers) or sharp for cutting (such as knives). In addition to being used for daily activities, stone tools were used throughout history for making statues and other celebratory objects. Over time, man improved the tools by adding elements such as handles and motors, and eventually metal tools replaced many of the early flint tools. Tools are examples of ways humans created solutions to challenges and situations they encountered in their daily lives. In early childhood classrooms, we use tools in much the same way.

Let's pretend for a moment that an art fairy came into your classroom one evening and took all of the writing and art tools. And let's further pretend that you cannot replace these missing tools because the early childhood catalog is lost and there is no extra money in the budget to spend. Yet it is important for children to have writing and art experiences the next morning. What would you do? Could you find a usable alternative for the missing tools, something similar in shape or size? Could these tools be made out of materials from nature? Could a suitable alternative be found at home, in a recycle shop, or in the garage?

Now, let's carry the story about the art fairy to the next level. Take all the paintbrushes from the easel or art area and store them away out of children's vision. Ask children to pretend along with you about the art fairy who stole the art tools. Challenge children's creativity and imagination by asking them to find, create, and use alternative paintbrushes. Perhaps some of the alternative paintbrushes you generate may come from nature. Here are some ideas of homemade tools to spur your imagination:

- Pine boughs or clumps of wheat grass tied together can replace a paintbrush.
- Sticks to draw in the sand or dirt take the place of writing implements and paper.
- Large, oblong, and smooth stones can be used to roll out clay. Also, fat sticks or buckeyes make good rolling pins for clay.
- A stone can be used to break open shells or seeds to see what's inside.
- Long grasses can be twisted together to make a string or rope to hold objects together.
- Various shapes of bark can be used to cut playdough or dig in the dirt.
- Natural sponges can be used as paintbrushes.
- Clam shells can be used to scoop sand or materials in the sensory table.

You will most likely find that you and the children can generate some amazing ideas. This experience

These paintbrushes were made using colorful cloth remnants attached to sticks.

may teach you a valuable lesson: You may not need commercially purchased art and writing tools. You may not need a lot of money. And you may be doing children a favor by hiding the paintbrushes.

After introducing children to these more primitive types of handmade tools, consider providing closely supervised experiences with and exposure to some of the following authentic tools, if appropriate and safe for the children's developmental levels:

- Hammer
- Wrench
- A level
- Nails
- A ruler
- Screwdriver
- A hand drill
- Measuring tape
- A shovel
- Safety goggles
- A clamp
- Carpenter's square
- Sandpaper
- A brace

Providing authentic tools means doing away with plastic and pretend tools purchased from an early childhood catalog or in the toy department of a children's store. Pretend tools are only for pretending. Because pretend tools are typically made of plastic, it is unrealistic to expect children to make anything substantial with them.

Offering real or authentic tools, on the other hand, honors children's capabilities and intelligence. Working with tools also gives children opportunities to practice self-regulation and self-control, as the consequences of misusing the tools are very real. Ultimately, by using authentic tools in the classroom, you are sending a message to children that they are competent and capable engineers and builders.

Tips for working with authentic tools:

- Have children wear safety goggles and gloves.
- Ask children to concentrate on using one tool at a time.
- Closely supervise the children's work.
- Prepare the environment.
- Limit the number of children participating.

Some teachers will not be willing to incorporate an authentic hammer and nails into the preschool classroom. You can still offer liquid glue to attach wood pieces together for stunning and equally gratifying results for young children.

Board of Jewish Early Education Centers at B'nai Tikvah (Deerfield, Illinois)

Music Making

In traditional cultures, music making is often an integral part of important group ceremonies such as weddings, initiation rites, and—believe it or not—preparation for battle. It has also been said that music making, which includes singing and dancing, fosters social connections and group bonding. Many instruments hold cultural and symbolic importance. For example, the ukulele from Hawaii, wood spoons from Russia, the didgeridoo from Australia, and the charango from Peru play significant roles in traditional arts and folk culture. Many of these ancient instruments were made from natural elements such as stones, clamshells, turtle shells, conch shells, cocoons, animal skins, wood, gourds, snake skin, beads, seeds, and nuts.

If you want to introduce children to these ancient and old-fashioned instruments, you could invite a musical historian from your community to share culturally influenced instruments or invite families to share and demonstrate the musical instruments of their culture that are meaningful to them. Find children's storybooks that include musical instruments too.

Drums. In many cultures, drums are an important part of life and ceremony. Make simple drums by decorating a coffee can or oatmeal container with construction paper or contact paper. Decorate with paint, markers, and stickers. Find images from the

Internet depicting a variety of drums of different sizes and shapes. Provide a selection of wooden dowels and spoons, rubber mallets, or sticks for the drumsticks.

Didgeridoo. A didgeridoo is a long wooden trumpet-like instrument originated by the aboriginal peoples of Australia. Used for 40,000 years, an authentic didgeridoo is made of a hollow wooden branch about five feet long with a beeswax mouthpiece. Because a didgeridoo is not commonly found everywhere, you can find pictures of the Didgeridoo on the Internet or check out library books to show children what the instrument looks like. You might also read the whimsical book *Do You Do a Didgeridoo?* by Nick Page. You can also find videos on YouTube (https://www.youtube.com/) that show the instrument being constructed and played, so give children a chance to hear authentic didgeridoo music.

Children can make a simplified version of the didgeridoo by using sections of PVC pipe (be sure to sand the edges) or cardboard tubes from wrapping paper. Just make sure the length is manageable (two to three feet) for the children. A small paper cone can be taped to one end to create a mouthpiece. Encourage children to decorate their didgeridoos by using paint, markers, and crayons. Other decorative elements— such as ribbons, yarn, or sequins—can be added to the instrument. To play the didgeridoo, a child should stand or sit with the instrument straight out in front of him, with one end resting on the ground. He can place

his mouth inside the tube and make a loose motorboat sound with his lips.

Maracas. Thought to have originated in Colombia more than 1,500 years ago, the maracas of today can be found in the orchestra's percussion section. Maracas are shaped much like baby rattles and make a similar sound. Original maracas were made from gourds. When the squash is picked and left to dry, the seeds separate from the hull and rattle when shaken. Another base for the instrument is a coconut shell emptied of its milk and filled with dried beans or lentils. Encourage children to find containers or objects that would make good maracas. For example, use two individual yogurt containers or paper cups that have been filled with rice or beans and taped together. To decorate the maracas, use tempera paint with liquid glue added or acrylic paint. Add fabric, twine, tissue paper, or tinfoil.

Rain stick. Legend has it that the Chilean Indians invented the rain stick to bring much needed moisture to their land. The authentic rain stick is like a tubular rattle and the cylinder is filled with cactus spines, bamboo or palm slivers, hard seeds, pebbles, beans, sand, rice, or tiny shells. The sounds created when these elements hit the cylinder mimic the sound of rain falling on the leaves.

Make a rain stick using a variety of sizes of cardboard tubes (such as paper towel, gift wrapping, mailing, or carpet rolls). Close off one end of the cardboard tube by taping paper over it. Once the one end of the tube is sealed, pour sand, rice, small pebbles, or a combination of elements into the tube. When you are satisfied with the sound, you can seal the other end of the tube with cardboard.

Tambourine. A tambourine is a common instrument in many cultures. You can very easily make one with children by using two paper plates that have been decorated with paint or markers. After the children are done decorating, encourage them to punch holes around the edges of the plates and place some small jingle bells on the top of one plate. Place the other plate over it with the two tops facing, and staple or glue them together. Then encourage the children to lace the top plate to the bottom by weaving the yarn in and out of the holes all around the plate. Once the child gets all the way around, tie off the yarn. Shake the hand-crafted tambourine to play it.

Storytelling

Children love to hear stories, and teachers love to tell stories. The challenge is finding stories about your community. How can you locate and identify them? Try starting a list of businesses that have been around your community for a long time. Make a few phone calls to see if the business owners have stories to tell about how and when the company started. Learn about the company's history, its founders, and mission. See if the owner

is willing to share photos and stories of the company building and its employees when it first opened. Ask if the children could tour the company and get a behind-the-scenes look at the operations. In the seaport of Baltimore, Maryland, for example, children could learn about an assembly line that makes fishing gear to serve people who fish for a living. In Kalamazoo, Michigan, children could learn about the manufacturing of paper, medicine, wagons, windmills, plows, and even mint extract and celery crops—which all helped to shape the city's past while leaving marks on the present. Learning about these companies and their history connects children to their community through stories about how people lived and worked in the past.

Another idea for storytelling is to connect with the local storytellers guild or call your city office to find out about storytelling festivals in your area. Connect with the community's senior citizen center or a member of the historical society who may be willing to share stories about their childhoods and perhaps pictures of the past. Children can also ask older relatives or friends to tell them a story about themselves. After children listen to the story, have an adult capture its essence by writing it down. These stories offer children knowledge of life and people in the past. Again, related pictures and images can help bring community memories to life for the children.

Actively participating in events such as parades or festivals is another way to become a part of community memories and stories. Here are some other ideas for connecting with the community's legacies:

- Ethnic organizations
- Libraries and museums
- Fraternal organizations
- Folklore and music societies (such as bluegrass pickers and gospel quartets)
- Cultural tourism organizations
- Festivals and craft fairs
- Church suppers
- Gardening and farmers groups
- Heritage preservation groups
- Hobby interest groups (such as quilting, knitting, and embroidering)

Folktales, which involve oral history passed down from generation to generation, are another kind of storytelling. Examples of books that share folktales are *Joseph Had a Little Overcoat* by Simms Taback and *Thunder Cake* by Patricia Polacco. Folktales are important because young children's identities are wrapped around the community and culture. Early childhood educators can support children by providing opportunities to become aware of the community's folk art, heritage, and traditions. Children also benefit by participating in traditions and rituals in their classroom community and creating their own.

Young children respond to community stories, memories, and authenticity in their lives, so find ways to infuse traditional arts into your classroom.

One strategy for infusing traditional arts is to offer children a designated area for a classroom workshop, where meaningful work can be done with authentic tools and materials. Some examples of workshops

On the Demise of the Vacant Lot

by Nancy Alexander, director, Northwestern State University's Children and Families Network

Growing up in the south, weather restrictions on outdoor play were minimal and usually were limited to occasional thunderstorms and a few heat-index-related issues. Our postwar subdivision filled with young families had a multitude of children. Bicycles, skates, and sidewalks expanded the neighborhood playmate options to a nine-to-twelve-square-block area.

The comfortable safety of such an environment meant that children could leave home early on a Saturday morning (or any day during long summer breaks) and spend the day somewhere in the neighborhood. Groups gathered at whichever house had the current favorite or newest toys, but interests could change quickly based on the ideas and whims of the players.

At noon, the accepted procedure was that wherever you were around lunchtime, you would be invited to eat, frequently that included a bowl of Campbell's tomato or chicken noodle soup with a peanut butter, cheese, or tuna sandwich. A quick phone call to home generated permission and often a reminder to come in by midafternoon if the temperature was high.

There was etiquette about this neighborhood roaming. One rule was that you did not go in someone's house if they were not home. Because people expected that the door might be unlocked, it was OK to open the door slightly, call "hello" or "is anybody home?" but never to step inside. And you played outdoors unless invited in by the mother. Before the common convenience of washers, dryers,

and vacuums, dirty kids were not always welcome inside.

Every neighborhood had a vacant lot—a place where you could often find playmates involved in an adventure of digging to the center of the earth (and yes, we thought we could!) or taking over the largest tree to install a tree house or tire swing. The abundance of pine straw or fall leaves provided ample resources and inspiration for pretend forts or clubhouses. If you were fortunate enough to have a blackberry patch, a thirty-minute group project picking berries meant that you might get to share a cobbler later. If you were really lucky, the ice cream truck would appear, and vanilla ice cream from Dixie Cups could top the cobbler. The Dixie Cup lids, with their movie star photos inside, became trading cards and collectibles. The small wooden spoons became props for doll play.

Part of the freedom we had was facilitated by a common southern architectural feature—the front porch. Caring, friendly adults sat on those porches on gliders or wooden swings, drinking iced tea and observing the neighborhood with watchful eyes. Everyone felt free to make sure that kid activities were in keeping with the neighborhood values. Neighbors went to school and church together, and belonged to scouts and fraternal groups together. Aunts, uncles, and cousins sometimes lived nearby. Children knew not only who lived in each house but also where each dog and cat belonged. In an era before leash laws, pets roamed freely right along with the children. Streetlights coming on at the end of the day signaled that it was time to head home, to either go inside for dinner or to continue playing in your own yard. A favorite task was to catch fireflies, competing to see who could catch the most, and then releasing them just prior to the inevitable call for a bath and bedtime.

Can we have such nostalgic experiences for children today? Considering the developed communities of patio homes, apartments, and carefully maintained common areas, where can a child dig or build a tree house? Or find a tire swing? The stuff of children's play is not attractive to many; homeowner associations might even impose fines or sanctions. In training I conduct for people who work with children, I often ask participants about their earliest memories of being outside as a child. No one has ever talked about an expensive piece of playground equipment at his or her school or park. Instead, the talk is usually about pine straw forts, backyard carnivals, or making mud pies. Many fondly remember activities in a neighborhood vacant lot. Yes, we need the good-quality equipment for gross motor activities, but we also need the natural materials and loose parts of those vacant lots that can be used in infinite, creative ways. Take, for example, a large cardboard box, the kind large appliances come

(continues)

in. Once any staples are removed, such boxes can become magic pieces of equipment that will keep children involved for days. Make friends with your local appliance store. People are very generous when they know that you want items for children—and after all, you're carrying off their discards.

Once we purchased a truckload of sand for a fall area and also needed to replenish a large sandbox in another area. That was the time I learned that the truck couldn't dump half in one location and half in another! A child bucket brigade worked for days carrying the sand one pail at a time to the sandbox. For adults, this might have been considered work and even drudgery, but for children it was challenging play with a purpose. Bring in a load of dirt or sand. The very experience of a dump truck delivery will be exciting for children. The dirt pile will stimulate many hours of play. Yes, children will get dirty, but a lawn sprinkler nearby can make short work of rinsing the dirt off. After all, in the summer children dry quickly. To me, there is something very pleasant about a dirty, sweaty, tired child because I know that child had a very good day.

Remember your own childhood. Think about that vacant lot and neighborhood where you lived. What are the memories that linger most with you? How can you provide those same memories for children today? Spend as much time as you can in the outdoors with children—build memories with them.

include weaver, florist, jeweler, artist, woodworker, tailor, and sculptor. Treat the space as you would any other learning center in the classroom by providing interesting materials that give children experience with hands-on, relevant, and productive work. Provide easily accessible materials and keep the area open and ready for the business of child play.

Creating Classroom Rituals and Traditions

Building a strong sense of classroom community begins with telling stories and creating memories. Stories are best told through rituals and traditions that connect children, families, and the community to the early childhood classroom. Note the difference, however, between classroom traditions and classroom rituals.

Rituals are actions that help provide predictability and structure to the child's day. They can help strengthen a child's sense of belonging and security. In an early childhood classroom, rituals might include singing the same traditional song each morning, welcoming each child with a high-five, or participating in the same attendance-taking procedure day after day. You might create a morning ritual, for example, by helping children make a commitment to say kind words or use gentle touches. Or you could begin the day with a quote and ask the children to express what it means to them. Using walking sticks is an example of a daily ritual. When the children arrive in the classroom, they find their own personally designed and constructed walking stick and move it to a designated spot. The transferring of the walking stick is a ritual denoting their important entry, the transition from the family to the classroom, and their presence in the classroom.

Early Learning Children's Community (East Lansing, Michigan)

In contrast, traditions revolve around history and culture. Our society is filled with traditional events—the annual neighborhood picnic, a father-daughter dance, a trip to the baseball field for opening day, a spaghetti dinner fundraiser at the neighborhood school, grandma's spring tea party with triangular-shaped sandwiches, a church or synagogue potluck dinner, and the family's turkey dinner with all its trimmings at the holidays. We attach special meaning to traditions.

Like the mortar holding bricks together, traditions provide a bridge connecting our important history with our even more important future. Likewise, early childhood classrooms need traditions to help connect the past to the present. Traditions such as the following help promote a sense of identity for those who are current residents and help them recognize the identity of community members who are now gone:

- A prekindergarten class collaborates to make a wreath made from natural found materials and hangs it in the entryway along with projects made by other graduates of the early childhood center.

The Adventure Club (Schererville, Indiana)

Rethinking the Classroom Landscape

- The director invites children and families to collaborate and make a cardboard weaving, which represents the center's community.

Encourage Explorations for the Future

Young children derive meaning from their surrounding environments and can better understand the link between the past and the present when there are visual reminders of what has transpired in the classroom, displays of completed and ongoing projects, and photographs of memories as well as images of recent experiences.

Although it is important to connect to the past, it is also equally important to illuminate the future. Too often we ask children for the facts, the proof of what they have learned in the past, so we can justify what should happen in the future. By doing so, we stifle their curiosity and problem-solving skills because the focus becomes reporting on the past rather than creating the future. As Gary Friedman, chairman and co-chief executive officer of Restoration Hardware, observes in his book *RH Objects of Curiosity*, "We begin to train ourselves to be historians rather than history makers. We become victims of other people's thinking instead of discovering and developing our own unique and authentic point of view. We search for certainty. And, by doing so we make certain the outcome of our journey will lack any sense of adventure

> " Knowledge can be a prison of the past, while curiosity can create a passion for the present and build a path to the future.
> —Gary Friedman,
> chairman of Restoration Hardware

or discovery." Although Friedman was referring to his company's team members and development of innovative hardware for the home, traditional early childhood environments also encourage children to live in the shadows of certainty. Filled with contemporary and commercially purchased materials and equipment, many early childhood environments lack physical artifacts that are reflective of the past. Because objects from the past are unfamiliar to children, they become objects of provocation and curiosity when placed in the classroom.

As teachers, it is our responsibility to transform cookie-cutter environments into places of wonder filled with evocative and unfamiliar objects, places of imagination and opportunities for problem solving, and places where children will remain forever curious. Our efforts can help shine a bright light on the past while also illuminating a new and reimagined view of what's ahead.

What's Your Classroom's Connection to the Past and Present?

Use this questionnaire to determine if your classroom is a place offering deep connections by representing the community's history, families' traditions, and traditions from long ago.

Directions: Select *A*, *B*, or *C* for each item listed below.

A = Strongly Agree

B = Agree

C = Strongly Disagree

_____ 1. We practice classroom rituals (songs, actions, pledges, or commitments) to promote a sense of community.

_____ 2. A designated and easily visible space connects children, their families, and traditions through images, stories, and artifacts.

_____ 3. Families and members from the community share stories, traditions, heritages, or knowledge of traditional arts (cooking, gardening, whittling, woodworking, basket making, and quilting).

_____ 4. Acknowledgment of the community's history, land, and people is made through center or classroom displays, children's artwork, scrapbooks, images, and artifacts.

_____ 5. At least two pieces of traditional or folk art reflective of the region or community (baskets, wood carvings, quilts, pressed flowers, musical instruments, sculptures, drums, pottery, textile weavings) are displayed in the center or classroom.

_____ 6. At least once a year, children participate in community events such as festivals, concerts, historical reenactments, or visit historical places such as local monuments, museums, or heritage preservation centers.

_____ 7. The classroom has a woodworking area and at least three real tools are included.

Scoring:

This tool helps assess how connected your classroom is to the past and present and if the community, children, and families are adequately connected to your classroom. Remember, the commitment to creating an environment that intentionally links the past to the present is an ongoing process of learning, so there is not one correct answer.

If you responded frequently with an *A*, you are well on your way to providing spaces that connect children and families to the community's history, traditions, and legacies.

If you responded frequently with a *B*, you may have some additional work to do to connect your classroom to the community's history, tradition, and legacies.

If you responded frequently with a *C*, you may want to consider implementing some of the ideas in this chapter to begin connecting your classroom to the community's history, tradition, and legacies.

A Final Invitation

- - - - - - - - - - - - - - - -

Earth and Sky, Woods and Fields, Lakes and Rivers, the Mountain and the Sea, are excellent
schoolmasters, and teach some of us more than we can ever learn in books.
—Sir John Lubbock, *The Use of Life*

Begin Designing Your New Landscape

Our goal in writing *Rethinking the Classroom Landscape* is to encourage you to think critically about early childhood environments and to offer ideas on how to transform your classroom into a reflective and meaningful landscape capable of reinforcing and enhancing young children's sense of belonging and connection to the environment, each other, their families, and community.

We intentionally designed this book so you would put it down, find inspiration, close the pages—and try a new idea or examine your classroom from a different perspective or never-before-considered angle. *Rethinking the Classroom Landscape* was written to be a continual resource and inspiration for you—a book with a cadre of ideas making you want to open its pages again and again when you need a fresh view. This book is meant to be dog-eared with important and personally relevant points highlighted or flagged with a sticky note.

The intention of this book is to give you pause—to make you think critically and honestly about your classroom. This book is intended to make you question why you do what you do when designing early childhood environments and how you might improve. Let this book challenge you, make you question, and inspire you to refresh and rewind how you think about early childhood environments.

We invite you to begin. Use this book as a starting point and a springboard to weave an environment vividly connecting children, adults, and their communities. Choose threads most meaningful to the children and families you serve—threads that reflect the community's topography, flora, and fauna as well as the people who live within the neighborhood. Deliberately incorporate each thread into your classroom's tapestry, allowing time for all your classroom inhabitants to fully embrace these important threads. Just as a lovingly and purposefully woven tapestry is made over a long period of time, creating a classroom landscape also takes time . . . and a concerted effort.

Think about what your classroom represents right now. Most likely, you have four walls, a few doors, some windows, and possibly children's bathrooms and storage areas to consider. After thinking about the examples and information presented in this book,

however, you know and understand a classroom to be much, much more. Through Bronfenbrenner's ecological theory of human development, you learned that the classroom landscape includes the human relationships and connections within and outside the classroom walls. And you also discovered how Newmark's five critical emotional needs have a powerful influence on children's growth and development. All these different environmental systems (family, school, and community) and individuals' needs interconnect to create the tapestry of young children's lives. When you promote Bronfenbrenner's interrelationships; magnify connections among the classroom, parents, neighborhood, and community; and incorporate Newmark's five critical emotional needs, the classroom's landscape is strengthened because you are making it more meaningful to young children.

Reflect on what you discovered in the informal assessments at the end of most chapters and how you

> "Children love to discover and create. Objects from nature offer more diversity in shape, texture, and visual appeal than any collection of store-bought toys. Out of sticks and stones can come mountains and cities.
> —**Molly Dannenmaier,** *A Child's Garden*

might improve your classroom landscape. This is a continual learning process.

It is our hope that after reading this book and seeing the beautiful images of classrooms across the nation, you will become newly inspired curators of your classroom landscapes. We invite you to abandon the notion of cookie-cutter or institutional environments and encourage opportunities for joyful expressions of uniqueness that each child and adult brings to the human landscape of your classroom. Because you are ultimately responsible for shaping the environment, be sure to create spaces where children feel welcome, included, and important, and experience a sense of belonging. Then you will have indeed created a beautiful tapestry. This is an invitation to begin.

References and Resources

References

Baker, Jennifer, and Laurie Mehalko. 1985. *Storybook Quilting*. Laverne, TN: Chilton.

Balagna, Mary, and Carol Babbitt. 2012. *Quilt It with Love: The Project Linus Story*. New York: Larks Crafts.

Barrett, Peter, and Lucinda Barrett. 2010. "The Potential of Positive Places: Senses, Brain, and Places." http://www.earthscan.co.uk/journal/inbi

Bartel, Marvin. 1999. "Art in Everyday Life." https://www.goshen.edu/art/ed/housetor.html

Berk, Laura. 1994. "Vygotsky's Theory: The Importance of Make-Believe Play." *Young Children*, 50(1): 30–39.

Bethmann, Laura. 2011. *Hand Printing from Nature*. North Adams, MA: Storey Publishing.

Boss, Bev. 1978. *Don't Move the Muffin Tin: A Hands-Off Guide to Art for the Young Child*. Carmichael, CA: Burton Gallery Publisher.

Boss, Bev. 1990. *Together We're Better: Establishing a Coactive Learning Environment*. Roseville, CA: Turn the Page Press.

Bronfenbrenner, Urie. 1979. *The Ecology of Human Development*. Cambridge, MA: Harvard University Press.

Bronfenbrenner, Urie. 1989. "Ecological Systems Theory." In Ross Vasta, ed. *Annals of Child Development* 6, 187–249. Greenwich, CT: JAI Press.

Bronfenbrenner, Urie. 1995. "Developmental Ecology through Space and Time: A Future Perspective." In Phyllis Moen, Glenn Elder Jr., and Kurt Luscher, eds., *Examining Lives in Context: Perspectives on the Ecology of Human Development*. Washington, DC: American Psychological Association.

Carson, Rachel. 1960. "Introduction." *Humane Biology Projects* [Pamphlet]. Washington, DC: Animal Welfare Institute.

Carson, Rachel. 1987. *The Sense of Wonder*. New York: HarperCollins.

Chawla, Louise. 1990. "Ecstatic Places." *Children's Environments Quarterly* 7(4): 18–23.

Clark, Alison. 2010. *Transforming Children's Spaces: Children's and Adults' Participation in Designing Learning Environments*. New York: Routledge Taylor & Francis Group.

Community Playthings. 2012. "Pre-K Spaces: Design for a Quality Classroom." *Community Playthings*. http://www.communityplaythings.com/resources/literature/booklets-and-cds/pre-k-spaces

Cox, Meg. 2012. *The Book of New Family Traditions: How to Create Great Rituals for Holidays and Every Day.* Philadelphia, PA: Running Press.

Cross, Aerial. 2012. *Nature Sparks: Connecting Children's Learning to the Natural World.* St. Paul, MN: Redleaf Press.

Curtis, Deb, and Margie Carter. 2003. *Designs for Living and Learning: Transforming Early Childhood Environments.* St. Paul, MN: Redleaf Press.

Daly, Lisa, and Miriam Beloglovsky. 2015. *Loose Parts: Inspiring Play in Young Children.* St. Paul, MN: Redleaf Press.

Dannenmaier, Molly. 1998. *A Child's Garden: Enchanting Outdoor Spaces for Children and Parents.* New York: Simon and Schuster.

Dannenmaier, Molly. 2008. *A Child's Garden: Sixty Ideas to Make any Garden Come Alive for Children.* Portland, OR: Timber Press.

Day, Christopher. 2007. *Environment and Children: Passive Lessons for the Everyday Environment.* New York: Architectural Press, Imprint of Routledge.

Deal, Terrence E., and Kent D. Peterson. 1999. *Shaping School Culture: The Heart of Leadership.* San Francisco, CA: Jossey-Bass.

DeViney, Jessica et al. 2010. *Inspiring Spaces for Young Children.* Beltsville, MD: Gryphon House.

Diehn, Gwen, and Terry Krautwurst. 1997. *Nature Crafts for Kids: 50 Fantastic Things to Make with Mother Nature's Help.* New York: Sterling Publishing Company, Inc.

Doorley, Scott, and Scott Witthoft. 2012. *Make Space: How to Set the Stage for Creative Collaboration.* Hoboken, NJ: John Wiley & Sons, Inc.

Dudek, Mark. 2005. *Children's Spaces.* Burlington MA: Architectural Press.

Dudek, Mark. 2013. *Nurseries: A Design Guide.* New York: Routledge.

Duncan, Sandra. 2010. "Gift of Nature." In *The Wisdom of Nature.* Ulster Park, NY: Community Playthings. http://www.communityplaythings.com/resources /articles/wisdomofnature/wisdom-of-nature.pdf

Duncan, Sandra. 2011. "Breaking the Code: Changing Our Thinking about Early Childhood Environments." *Exchange* 200: 13–16.

Duncan, Sandra. 2015. "Lessons from the Bowerbird: How to Create Appealing, Beautiful, and Purposeful Habitats." *Community Playthings,* http://www.communityplaythings.com/resources /articles/2015 bower-bird

Duncan, Sandra, Jessica DeViney, and Sara Harris. 2010. "Nature Swap: Art Tools Go GREEN!" *Exchange:* 60–64.

Duncan, Sandra, and Mickey MacGillivray. 2014, November/December. "Metal: A Perfect Play Material for Children's Improvisation." *Exchange* 57–60.

Duncan, Sandra, and Michelle Salcedo. 2012. "Are Your Children in Times Square? Moving from Sensory Overload to Sensory Engagement." *Exchange* 208: 48–52.

Duncan, Sandra, and Michelle Salcedo. 2014. "Are Your Children in Times Square? Moving from Confinement to Engagement." *Exchange* 221: 26–29.

Editors of Teaching Young Children. 2015. *Expressing Creativity in Preschool*. Washington, DC: National Association for the Education of Young Children.

Environmental Protection Agency. 2014. "Basic Information. IAQ Design Tools for Schools." Accessed September 20, 2015. http://www.epa.gov/iaq/schooldesign/introduction.html

Fagan, Aimee. 2015. *Sewing in the Montessori Classroom: A Practical Life Curriculum*. Charlottesville, VA: Aimee Fagan.

Fishbaugh, Angela. 2011. *Celebrate Nature! Activities for Every Season*. St. Paul, MN: Redleaf Press.

Friedman, Gary. 2014. *RH Objects of Curiosity*. Corte Madera, CA: Restoration Hardware.

Gardner, Howard. 2011. *Truth, Beauty, and Goodness Reframed: Educating for the Virtues of the Twenty-First Century*. New York: Basic Books.

Grande, John K. 2004. *Art Nature Dialogues: Interviews with Environmental Artists*. Albany, NY: State University of New York Press.

Green, Carie. 2011. "A Place of My Own: Exploring Preschool Children's Special Places in the Home Environment." *Children, Youth, and Environment* 21(2): 118–144.

Greenman, Jim. 1992. "Places for Childhoods: How Institutional Are You?" *Exchange* 87: 49–52.

Greenman, Jim. 1998. *Places for Childhoods: Making Quality Happen in the Real World*. Redmond, WA: Exchange Press.

Greenman, Jim. 2004. "The Experience of Space, the Pleasure of Place." *Exchange* 155, 36–37.

Greenman, Jim. 2005. *Caring Spaces, Learning Spaces: Children's Environments That Work*. Redmond, WA: Exchange Press.

Greenspan, Stanley, and Nancy T. Greenspan. 1989. *First Feelings: Milestones in the Emotional Development of Your Baby and Child*. New York: Penguin Group.

Greenspan, Stanley, and Nancy Lewis. 1999. *Building Healthy Minds: The Six Experiences That Create Intelligence and Emotional Growth in Babies and Young Children*. Cambridge, MA: Da Capo Press.

Gussow, Alan. 1972. *A Sense of Place: The Artist and the American Land*. San Francisco, CA: Friends of the Earth.

Hall, Ellen L., and Jennifer K. Rudkin. 2011. *Seen and Heard: Children's Rights in Early Childhood Education*. New York: Teachers College Press.

Holman, Cas. 2012. "The Case for Letting Kids Design Their Own Play." *Fast Company*. http://www.fastcodesign.com/3048508/the-case-for-letting-kids-design-their-own-play

Horne Martin, Sandra. 2002. "The Classroom Environment and Its Effects on the Practice of Teachers." *Journal of Environmental Psychology* 22: 139–56.

Howell, Jacky, and Kimberly Reinhard. 2015. *Rituals and Traditions: Fostering a Sense of Community in Preschool*. Washington, DC: National Association for the Education of Young Children.

Howes, Carollee, Deborah Phillips, and Marcy Whitebrook. 1992. "Thresholds of Quality: Implication for the Social Development of Children in Center-Based Care." Child Development 63(2): 449–460.

Isabell, Rebecca, and Pamela Evanshen. 2012. *Real Classroom Makeovers: Practical Ideas for Early Childhood Classrooms*. Beltsville, MD: Gryphon House.

Korpela, Kalevi. 2002. "Children's Environment." In *Handbook of Environmental Psychology*, edited by Robert Bechtel and Arza Churchman, 363–73. New York: John Wiley & Sons.

Kuh, Lisa P. 2014. *Thinking Critically about Environments for Young Children: Bridging Theory and Practice*. New York: Teachers College Press, Columbia University.

Lester, Stephen, Michael Schade, and Caitlin Weingand. 2008. *Volatile Vinyl: The New Shower Curtain's Chemical Smell*. Falls Church, VA: Center for Health Environment and Justice.

Levin, Susan, and Gloria Tracy. 2007. *Show Me How: Quilting: Quilting Storybooks and How-to-Quilt Instructions*. New York: Sixth & Spring Books.

Louv, Richard. 2006. *Last Child in the Woods*. Chapel Hill, NC: Algonquin Books.

Lovejoy, Sharon. 1999. *Roots, Shoots, Buckets, and Boots: Gardening Together with Children*. New York: Workman Publishing Company, Inc.

Lovejoy, Sharon. 2001. *Sunflower Houses: A Book for Children and Their Grown-Ups*. New York: Workman.

Lubbock, John. 1895. *The Use of Life*. New York: Macmillan.

Lutts, Ralph. 1985. "Place, Home, and Story in Environmental Education." *Journal of Environmental Education* 17(1): 37–41.

Martin, Jody. 2011. *Preschool Health and Safety Matters*. Silver Spring, MD: Gryphon House.

Maslow, Abraham. 1954. *Towards a Psychology of Being*. New York: Van Nostrand.

Maslow, Abraham. 1968. *Toward a Psychology of Being*. New York: D. VanNostrand.

Maslow, Abraham. 1971. *The Farther Reaches of Human Nature*. New York: Viking Press.

McAuliffe, Gillian. 2009. *The Humble Honky Nut: Awakening Relationships with Nature through Indoor Environments*. Churchlands, WA: Bold Park Community School Outreach.

Morehouse, Paul. 2013. "The Importance of Music Making in Child Development." *YC: Young Children* 68(4): 82–89.

Morrow, Lesley. 1990. "Preparing the Classroom Environment to Promote Literacy during Play." *Early Childhood Research Quarterly* 5: 537–534.

Nabhan, Gary, and Stephen Trimble. 1995. *The Geography of Childhood: Why Children Need Wild Places*. Boston, MA: Beacon Press.

National Scientific Council on the Developing Child. 2011. *A Decade of Science Informing Policy: The Story of the National Scientific Council on the Developing Child.* Cambridge, MA: Harvard University.

Newmark, Gerald. 2008. *How to Raise Emotionally Healthy Children—Meeting the Five Critical Needs of Children and Parents Too!* Tarzana, CA: NMI Publishers.

Nicholson, Simon. 1974. "How Not to Cheat Children: The Theory of Loose Parts." *Landscape Architecture,* 62(1): 30–34.

Olds, Anita. 2001. *Child Care Design Guide.* New York: McGraw-Hill.

Oliver, Sharon, and Edgar Klugman. 2002. "What We Know about Play." *Child Care Information Exchange,* 16–18.

Olmsted, Sarah. 2012. *Imagine Childhood: Exploring the World through Nature, Imagination, and Play – 25 Projects That Spark Curiosity and Adventure.* Boston, MA: Roost Books.

Page, Nick. 2008. *Do You Do a Didgeridoo?* Berkhamsted, UK: Make Believe Ideas.

Paley, Vivian. 2004. *A Child's Work: The Importance of Fantasy Play.* Chicago, IL: University of Chicago Press.

Pelo, Ann. 2013. *The Goodness of Rain: Developing an Ecological Identity in Young Children.* Redmond, WA: Exchange Press.

Peterson, Elizabeth. 1996. *The Changing Faces of Tradition: A Report on the Folk and Traditional Arts in the United States.* Washington, DC: National Endowment for the Arts.

Pica, Rae. 2003. *Your Active Child. How to Boost Physical, Emotional, and Cognitive Development through Age-Appropriate Activity.* New York: McGraw-Hill.

Pica, Rae. 2015. *What if Everybody Understood Child Development?* Thousand Oaks, CA: Corwin.

Prescott, Elizabeth. "The Physical Environment: A Powerful Regulator of Experience." *Exchange* 100(2): 9–15.

Rivkin, Mary. 1995. *The Great Outdoors: Restoring Children's Right to Play Outside.* Washington, DC: National Association for the Education of Young Children.

Sherwood, P. 2004. *The Healing Art of Clay Therapy.* Melbourne, Australia: ACER Press.

Sobel, David. 2002. *Children's Special Places: Exploring the Role of Forts, Dens, and Bush Homes in Middle Childhood.* Detroit, MI: Wayne State University Press.

Stewart, Deborah. 2010. "The Child's View of Your Early Childhood Classroom." *Teach Preschool,* http://www.teachpreschool.org/2010/07/the-childs-eye-view-of-your-early-childhood-classroom/Stoecklin, Vicki. 2001. The Role of Culture in Designing Child Care Facilities." *Exchange* 139: 60–63.

Sutton, Mary Jo. 2011. "In the Hands and Mind: The Intersection of Loose Parts and Imagination in Evocative Settings for Young Children." *Children, Youth and Environment* 21(2): 409–424.

Tarr, Patricia. 2004. *Consider the Walls: Beyond the Journal: Young Children on the Web.* Washington, DC: National Association for the Education of Young Children.

Topal, Cathy, and Lella Gandini. 1999. *Beautiful Stuff! Learning with Found Materials.* Worcester, MA: Davis Publications, Inc.

Tuan, Yi-Fu. 1977. *Space and Place: The Perspective of Experience.* Minneapolis, MN: University of Minnesota Press.

U.S. Census Bureau. 2013. American Community Survey. http://factfinder2.census.gov/faces/nav/jsf/pages/index.xhtml

Walsh, Glenda, and John Gardner. 2005. "Assessing the Quality of Early Years Learning Environments." *Early Childhood Research and Practice* 7(1): 1–18.

Wheatley, Margaret, and Myron Kellner-Rogers. 1998. *A Simpler Way.* San Francisco, CA: Berrett-Koehler Publishers, Inc.

Wilson, Ruth. 2010. "Aesthetics and Sense of Wonder." *Exchange* 193: 24–26.

Wilson, Ruth. 2014. "Beauty in the Lives of Young Children." *Exchange* 216: 36.

Wilson, Ruth. 2014. "Honoring the Essential Self." *Exchange* 211: 16.

Wilson, Ruth. 2016. *Learning Is in Bloom.* Lewisville, NC: Gryphon House.

Wiseman, Ann Sayre, and John Langstaff. 2003. *Making Music: From Tambourines to Rain Sticks to Dandelion Trumpets, Walnut Castanets to Shepherd's Pipes to an Abundance of Homemade Drums.* North Adams, MA: Storey Publishing.

Zane, Linda. 2015. *Pedagogy and Space: Design Inspirations for Early Childhood Classrooms.* St. Paul, MN: Redleaf Press.

Recommended Children's Storybooks and Reference Books

Animals

Annie and the Wild Animals by Jan Brett

Life Size Zoo by Kristin Earhart

Growing Frogs by Vivian French

Animal Tracks: Wild Poems to Read Aloud by Charles Ghigna

The Good Luck Cat by Joy Harjo

And So They Build by Bert Kitchen

Charlie the Ranch Dog by Reed Rummond

Thanks to the Animals by Allen Sockabasin-Passamaquoddy

Art

The Art Lesson by Tomie dePaola

Harold and the Purple Crayon by Crockett Johnson

Art by Patrick McDonnell

My First ABC by the Metropolitan Museum of Art

I Spy Colors in Art by Lucy Micklethwait

Patrick Paints a Picture by Saviour Pirotta

Jingle Dancer by Cynthia Leitich Smith

Mouse Paint by Ellen Stoll Walsh

Birds

Fine Feathered Friends: All About Birds by Tish Rabe

First the Egg by Laura Vaccaro Seeger

More by I. C. Springman

Rainbow Crow by Nancy Van Laan

Families

My Family by Debbie Bailey

Kumak's House—A Tale of the Far North by
    Michael Bania

The First Strawberries—A Cherokee Story, retold by
    Joseph Bruchac

Do You Want to Be My Friend? by Eric Carle

Dog and Bear: Two Friends, Three Stories by Laura
    Vaccaro Seeger

Folk Tales, Legends, Traditional Arts

The Legend of the Indian Paintbrush by Tomie dePaola

The Legend of the Bluebonnet by Tomie dePaola

The Quilt Story by Tony Johnston and Tomie dePaola

The Three Little Pigs by Paul Galdone

Humpty Who? by Jennifer Griffin

Pocketful of Posies by Salley Mavor

The Fire Children: A West African Folk Tale by
    Eric Maddern

Anansi the Spider: A Tale from the Ashanti by
    Gerald McDermott

*Can You Guess My Name? Traditional Tales around the
    World* by Judy Sierra

Gardens

The Enormous Potato by Aubrey Davis

Eating the Alphabet: Fruits and Vegetables from A to Z by
    Lois Ehlert

Apples by Jacqueline Farmer

From Seed to Plant by Gail Gibson

Mrs. Spitzer's Garden by Edith Pattou

The Giant Carrot by Jan Peck

How Plants Grow by Dona Herweek Rice

Rah, Rah, Radishes! A Vegetable Chant by
    April Pulley Sayre

Berry Magic by Teri Sloat and Betty Huffmon

*Carlos and the Squash Plant / Carlos y la Planta de
    Calbaza* by Jan Romero Stevens

Pumpkin, Pumpkin by Jeanne Titherington

Geology and Topography

Anno's Counting Book by Mitsumasa Anno

*The People of Cascadia—Pacific Northwest Native
    American History* by Heidi Bohan

*Geology of the Great Plains and Mountain West:
    Investigate How the Earth Was Formed* by Cynthia
    Light Brown

*Geology of the Eastern Coast: Investigate How the
    Earth Was Formed* by Cynthia Light Brown and
    Kathleen Brown

This Place Is Cold (Imagine Living Here) by Vicki Cobb

This Place Is Crowded: Japan (Imagine Living Here) by
    Vicki Cobb

This Place Is Dry: Arizona's Sonoran Desert (Imagine
    Living Here) by Vicki Cobb

This Place Is High: The Andes Mountains of South America (Imagine Living Here) by Vicki Cobb

This Place Is Lonely: The Australian Outback (Imagine Living Here) by Vicki Cobb

This Place Is Wild: East Africa (Imagine Living Here) by Vicki Cobb

My Arctic 1, 2, 3 by Michael Arvaarluk Kusugak

National Geographic Kids Everything Rocks and Minerals by Steve Tomecek

Three Bears of the Pacific Northwest by Marcia and Richard Vaughan

Way Up in the Arctic by Jennifer Ward

Grounding

From the Ground Up by Laura Koniver

Giving Thanks—A Native American Good Morning Message by Chief Jake Swamp

Nature

The Very Hungry Caterpillar by Eric Carle

Science Kids Plant Patterns by Aaron Carr

Outside Your Window: A First of Nature by Nicola Davies

And Then It's Spring by Julie Fogliano

The Vegetables We Eat by Gail Gibbons

These books are part of the Nature Upclose series by John Himmelman

> *A Dandelion's Life*
>
> *A House Spider's Life*
>
> *A Hummingbird's Life*
>
> *A Ladybug's Life*

A Monarch Butterfly's Life

A Slug's Life

A Wood Frog's Life

An Earthworm's Life

Over and Under the Snow by Kate Messner

Who Loves the Fall by Bob Raczka

Just A Walk by Jordan Wheeler

Ocean, Water, and Rain

Seashells by the Seashore by Marianne Berkes

Exploring Water with Young Children by Ingrid Chalufour and Karen Worth

The Pond Book by Karen Dawe

How Many Snails? A Counting Book by Paul Giganti Jr.

Wave by Suzy Leel

The Magic Fish by Freya Littledale

Puddles by Jonathan London

Little Shark by Annie Rockwell

Rain Talk by Mary Serfozo

How to Cross a Pond: Poems about Water by Marilyn Singer

W Is for Waves: An Ocean Alphabet by Marie and Roland Smith

Rocks

Stone Soup by Marcia Brown

If You Find a Rock by Peggy Christian

Rocks Not Happy in Sacks by Gilbert Walking Bull and Sally Moore

Shadows

Moonbear's Shadow by Frank Asch
What Makes a Shadow? by Clyde Robert Bulla

Social/Emotional Health

Families (Our Global Community) by Lisa Easterling
A Rainbow of Friends by P. K. Hallinan
Owen and Mzee: The True Story of a Remarkable Friendship by Isabella Hatkoff, Craig Hatkoff, and Paula Kahumbu
The Invisible String by Patrice Karst
The Color of Us by Karen Kutz
Little Blue and Little Yellow by Leo Lionni
Someday by Alison McGhee
Families by Anne Morris
What I Like about Me by Allia Zobel Nolan
It's Okay to Be Different by Todd Parr

Kissing Hand by Audrey Penn
A Pocket Full of Kisses by Audrey Penn
The Human Alphabet by Pilobolus
The Skin You Live In by Michael Tyler
City Dog, Country Frog by Mo Willems

Trees

Northwest Trees by Stephen F. Arno and Ramona P. Hammerly
A Seed Is Sleepy by Dianna Hutts Aston
The Great Kapok Tree by Lynne Cherry
Leaf Man by Lois Ehlert
Red Leaf, Yellow Leaf by Lois Ehlert
Field Guides—Trees by Maria Angeles Julivert
Why Do Leaves Change Color? by Betsy Maestro
Red Sings from Treetops: A Year in Colors by Joyce Sidman
The Giving Tree by Shel Silverstein
The Busy Tree by Jennifer Ward

Teacher Resource Books

Hand Printing from Nature by Laura Bethmann
Creating the Peaceable Classroom by Sandy Bothmer
Touchpoints: The Essential Reference Guide: Your Child's Emotional and Behavioral Development by T. Berry Brazelton
From My Side: Being a Child by Sylvia Chard and Yvonne Kogan
Children, Spaces, Relations: Metaproject for an Environment for Young Children by Reggio Children and Domus Academy Research Center

Childspaces 2: Another Design Sourcebook for Early Childhood Environments by Toni Christie and Robin Christie
The Ecology of Imagination in Childhood by Edith Cobb
Pre-K Spaces—Design for a Quality Classroom published by Community Playthings
The Stuff of Childhood—Play Equipment to Support Early Education published by Community Playthings
The Wisdom of Nature—Out of My Back Door published by Community Playthings

Sharing Nature with Children by Joseph Cornell

A Child's Garden: Enchanting Outdoor Spaces for Children and Parents by Molly Dannenmaier

S•E•T Social Emotional Tools for Life: An Early Childhood Teacher's Guide to Supporting Strong Emotional Foundations and Successful Social Relationships by Michelle Forrester and Kay Albrecht

Play and Playscapes by Joe Frost

Emotional Intelligence by Daniel Goleman

Caring Spaces, Learning Places: Children's Environments That Work by Jim Greenman

Edge: An Environmentally Appropriate Early Childhood Curriculum by Mercy Hernandez and I Irma Gómez

Early Learning Environments That Work by Rebecca Isbell

Real Classroom Makeovers: Practical Ideas for Early Childhood Classrooms by Rebecca Isbell and Pamela Evansham

Natural Playscapes: Creating Outdoor Play Environments for the Soul by Rusty Keeler

Communication Friendly Spaces Approach—Rethinking Learning Environments for Children and Families by Elizabeth Jarman

Lessons from Turtle Island—Native Curriculum for Early Childhood Classrooms by Guy Jones and Sally Moomaw

The Nature Connection an Outdoor Workbook for Kids, Families and Classrooms by Clare Walker Leslie

Educating from the Heart—Theoretical and Practical Approaches to Transforming Education edited by A. Johnson and M. Webb Neagley

Cultivating Outdoor Classrooms by Eric Nelson

Bring the Outdoors In: Garden Projects for Decorating and Styling Your Home by Shane Powers

Master Players: Learning from Children at Play by Gretchen Reynolds and Elizabeth Jones

Steps to a Bountiful Kids Garden by the National Gardening Association

Easy Garden Projects to Make, Build, and Grow by Barbara Pleasant (Yankee Magazine)

Heart-Centered Teaching Inspired by Nature by Nancy Rosenow

The North Atlantic Coast: A Literary Field Guide, edited by Sara St. Antoine

The South Atlantic Coast and Piedmont: A Literary Field Guide edited by Sara St. Antoine

The California Coast: A Literary Field Guide edited by Sara St. Antoine

The Great Lakes: A Literary Field Guide edited by Sara St. Antoine

Neurons to Neighborhoods by Jack Shonkoff and Deborah Phillips

Hollyhocks and Honeybees: Garden Projects for Young Children by Sara Starbuck, Marla Olthof, and Karen Midden

Kids' Easy-to-Create Wildlife Habitats: For Small Spaces in City-Suburbs by Emily Stetson

I Love Dirt! Fifty-Two Activities to Help You and Your Kids Discover the Wonders of Nature by Jennifer Ward

Nurture through Nature: Working with Children under 3 in Outdoor Environments by Claire Warden

Our Peaceful Classroom by Aline Wolf

Connecting: Friendship in the Lives of Young Children and Their Teachers by Dennie Palmer Wolf and Bonnie Neugebauer

Coyote's Guide to Connecting with Nature by Jon Young, Ellen Haas, and Evan McGowan

Organizations and Websites
Alliance for Childhood

www.allianceforchildhood.org

The Alliance for Childhood promotes policies and practices that support children's healthy development, love of learning, and joy in living. Our public education campaigns bring to light both the promise and the vulnerability of childhood. We act for the sake of the children themselves and for a more just, democratic, and ecologically responsible future.

American Folklore Society

www.afsnet.org

The American Folklore Society is an association of folklorists: people who study and communicate knowledge about folklore throughout the world.

The Butterfly Website

http://butterflywebsite.com/butterflygardening.cfm

Tips, ideas, and inspiration for creating your own beautiful butterfly garden. Educational features, images, and more!

Children and Nature Network

www.childrenandnature.org

This network was created to encourage and support the people and organizations working to reconnect children with nature. It provides a critical link between researchers and individuals, educators and organizations dedicated to children's health and well-being. Let's G.O. (Get Outside) is a youth-inspired organization, which is part of Children and Nature Network, to rally people of diverse backgrounds and ages to get outside and spend time in nature.

Community Playthings

www.communityplaythings.com

Website offers high-quality equipment, but also provides resources for the early childhood practitioner including a library of free articles, booklets, and training videos.

Coyote Trails School of Nature

www.coyotetrails.org

Instructors are trained to live in the wilderness. The curriculum involves skills and traditions, known as *primitive living skills*, from indigenous cultures around the world. Students have opportunities to experience new adventures and gain an appreciation of the natural world while gaining self-reliance and confidence.

Design Share

www.designshare.com/

Website is focused on the best in education facilities and their impact on the learning process.

Discount School Supply

www.discountschoolsupply.com

This school supply company offers a couple choices for children to practice the traditional art of weaving on a loom. They offer a Classroom Loom (#STLOOM) for children to work on collaboratively or they offer a Beginner's Wooden Loom (#RLOOM) that they can work on individually.

EmotionallyHealthyChildren.org

www.emotionallyhealthychildren.org

This website provides tools for teachers and parents working with children in supporting children's emotional health.

Green Hearts Institute for Nature in Childhood

www.greenheartsinc.org

Provides ten design elements and guidelines for nature play spaces in nature centers and other natural areas.

International Play Association

www.ipausa.org

This association aims to protect, preserve, and promote the child's right to play. Specific interests include environments for play emphasizing universal access, leisure time facilities, programs that develop the whole child, play leadership training, toys, and play materials.

Kaplan Early Learning Company

www.kaplanco.com/

Website offers weaving looms, wood blocks and furniture, classroom and play materials, and curriculum and professional development resources.

Kids Matter

www.kidsmatter.edu.au

Developing a sense of cultural identity supports the development of your child's identity and self-esteem, as well as their feeling of belonging to their community. These are all protective factors for mental health and well-being in early childhood. Children's cultural identity develops through language, storytelling, relationships, and traditions and routines. You can help your children to connect with their heritage by sharing cultural stories and practices.

Let the Children Play

www.letthechildrenplay.net

Let the Children Play celebrates the importance of play in the lives and education of our children by sharing my own experiences in a play-based preschool and providing inspiration, tips, and information to help parents and teachers alike put the play back into childhood.

Life without Plastic

www.lifewithoutplastic.com

This website offers safe, high-quality, ethically sourced, earth-friendly alternatives to plastic products.

National Congress of American Indians

www.ncai.org/tribal-directory

Tribal directory for tribes located within the United States of America. Tribal contact information listed by state, a resource for locating tribal groups in your area for educational and historical presentations.

National Council for the Traditional Arts

http://ncta-usa.org

The National Council for the Traditional Arts is a corporation dedicated to the presentation and documentation of traditional arts in the United States. Its purpose is to share the cultural riches of our diverse nation, as well as celebrate and honor the keepers of this priceless heritage.

National Geographic

www.nationalgeographic.com

This website offers multimedia kits focused on nature such as A Tree through the Seasons, Why Does It Rain?, The Sun, the Moon, and What Happens in Winter?

National Museum of the American Indian

www.nmai.si.edu

You can learn more about Native American traditions, history, and contemporary issues, or explore resources for the classroom at this site.

National Wildlife Federation

www.nwf.org

The National Wildlife Federation's Be Out There is a national movement to give back to American children what they don't even know they've lost—their connection to the natural world. With a wealth of activities, events, and resources, Be Out There reconnects families with the great outdoors to raise happy, healthy children with a life-long love of nature.

Natural Learning Initiative

www.naturalearning.org

The Natural Learning Initiative, founded in 2000 with the purpose of promoting the importance of the natural environment in the daily experience of all children, through environmental design, action research, education, and dissemination of information, is a research and professional development unit at the College of Design, NC State University.

Natural Pod

www.naturalpod.com

This company offers beautifully manufactured equipment for the early childhood classroom while promoting natural play through naturally inspired environments.

Natural Start Alliance

www.naturalstart.org

The Natural Start Alliance is a network dedicated to helping young children experience and care for nature.

Nature Action Collaborative for Children

www.worldforumfoundation.org

Nature Action Collaborative for Children is an initiative of the World Forum Foundation with the mission of reconnecting children with the natural world by making developmentally appropriate nature education a sustaining and enriching part of the daily lives of the world's children.

Nature Explore

www.natureexplore.org

Nature Explore is a collaborative program of the Arbor Day Foundation and Dimensions of Educational Research Foundation. Through design services, workshops, and natural products, they support your efforts to transform children's daily lives through connections with nature.

Photos to Art

www.art.com/photostoart/

The Photos [to] Art website helps turn personal photos of people, places, and memories into custom art in just a few minutes.

Project Learning Tree

www.plt.org

Created by Project Learning Tree, an award-winning environmental education program for teachers, this website provides ideas for hands-on experiences with trees and nature for young children.

Teaching Tolerance

www.tolerance.org/publication /family-and-community-engagement

Incorporating family and community knowledge enhances student learning. Students possess tremendous experiential wisdom on issues related to identity, culture, history, and justice. Parents, grandparents, aunts, uncles, friends, cousins, neighbors, and community leaders frequently have stories to share about their lives and perspectives.

Wilderness Awareness School

www.wildernessawareness.org

Wilderness Awareness School's approach to nature education draws upon the vast experiences of naturalists and indigenous peoples from around the world.

Index

M

N

O

objects, authentic, 101–102

"Our memories" activity, 19

outdoor area, 86–89

outdoors, 3, 87–90, 122–177. see also nature; topography

P

past, connection to, 199, 201, 228–229. see also arts, traditional

patience, and nature, 78

peak experiences, 178, 180

Pelo, Ann, 168

Penix, Sue, 134, 193

Peterson, Elizabeth, 200

Pica, Rae, 125

place

    classroom as, 84

    creating, 79, 81–82

    described, 80

    and identity, 168, 178, 180

    outdoor area, 86–89

    power of, 77, 79

    sense of, 77, 79

    vs. space, 79–80, 116–117

    transforming classroom into, 91–117

"Places for Childhoods" (Greenman), 38

plants, for gardens, 139–141

plastic, 50–53, 60, 65

plastic bag replacement project, 60

play, 3, 165

playdough, 158, 160–161

playground, natural, 165

Polacco, Patricia, 221

porches, 223

Potter, Mari, 179

practices of commitment, 200

Pratt, Caroline, 190

predictability, 225

preschools, nature-based, 64

present, 178

    connection to, 199, 201, 228–229 (see also arts, traditional)

problem solving, 78

puddles, 166–167

pumpkins, 140–141

Q

questionnaires

    children's experience with earthing, 194–195

    classroom's connection to past and present, 228–229

    classroom tapestry, 30–31

    plastic inventory, 52

    space vs. place, 116–117

quilt making, 201–204